D1478521

Hope Emily Allen

Medieval Scholarship and Feminism

Hope Emily Allen in London in the early 1920s.

Hope Emily Allen

Medieval Scholarship
and Feminism

John C. Hirsh

Pilgrim Books
Norman, Oklahoma
73070

Other Books by John C. Hirsh

Medieval Manuscripts in Lehigh University Libraries

Barlam and Iosaphat, A Middle English Life of Buddha. Early English Text Society, OS 290

The Revelations of Margery Kempe: Paramystical Practices in Late-Medieval England

Library of Congress Cataloging-in-Publication Data

Hirsh, John C.
    Hope Emily Allen : medieval scholarship and feminism / John C.
Hirsh.
        p.   cm.
    Bibliography: p.
    Includes index.
    ISBN 0-937664-80-4 : $33.95
    1. Allen, Hope Emily. 2. Anglicists—United States—Biography.
3. Medievalists—United States—Biography.   4. Feminists—United
States—Biography.   5. English literature—Middle English,
1100–1500—Study and teaching—United States.   6. Christian
literature, English (Middle)—Study and teaching—United States.
I. Title.
PE64.A59H67   1988
820'.9'001—dc19
    [B]   88-17809
                                                              CIP

Copyright © 1988 by Pilgrim Books, P.O. Box 2399, Norman, Oklahoma 73070

ISBN: 0-937664-80-4

For my sisters

TABLE OF CONTENTS

FOREWORD

O ne of the great pleasures I have had in writing this book has been
the people I have met while I have been doing so. Hope Allen's
family has given me every possible assistance, and it is to them
that I am particularly indebted. Her nephew, Mr. Henry G. Allen, and
his wife, Mrs. Mildred Gorman Allen, have allowed me access to family
papers, answered numerous questions, and given me gracious hospitality
during my visits to Oneida. Mr. Allen's sister, Mrs. Harriet Allen Kerr,
who accompanied her aunt to Europe after graduation and knew her from
childhood, and her husband, Dr. Albert Kerr, discussed Hope Allen with
me, providing many useful insights. Mrs. Florence Boyd Allen, who
knew Hope very well during her last years, and Mrs. Jane Kinsley Rich
likewise provided sensitive, useful information.

I am indebted to Mrs. Nita S. Baugh for extending me many courtesies
while this book was in progress and for sharing her specialist knowledge in
the areas in which both she and Hope Allen were expert. Professor Ruth
Dean and Dr. Ian Doyle, both of whom understood Hope's work, and
either knew or corresponded with her, provided marked assistance, as did
Mrs. Margaret Ogden, of Ann Arbor, Michigan.

My work at Bryn Mawr was greatly assisted by Ms. Lucy West, the
College Archivist, who expedited my examination of relevant papers and
documents and provided me with expert advice about Bryn Mawr in
Hope's day. In Bryn Mawr too I was graciously received by Professor
Charles Mitchell and his wife, Jean Flower Mitchell.

In London I was generously assisted by Mr. Marco Pallis, the explorer,
Buddhologist, and musician, and by Mr. John Cressey, of Dr. Williams's
Theological Library; Dr. Elizabeth M. Hallam, of the Public Record

Office; and Miss K. J. Wallace, Archivist of the British Library. I have received further assistance from Miss A. Phillips, of Newnham College, Cambridge; Ms. Jane S. Knowles, of Radcliffe College Archives; Professor Robert Lewis and Professor Richard W. Bailey, of the University of Michigan; Mr. Daniel Traistor, of the University of Pennsylvania Library; and Mr. Mark Weimer, of Syracuse University Library. I have had help from Sister Anna Maria, O.Ss.S., Abbess of Syon Abbey, in South Brent, Devon, and from Dom Louis Soltner, O.S.B., of the Abbey of Saint Pierre de Solesmes, where the early Farnborough archives were transferred in 1947.

At Oxford, Professor Douglas Gray invited a seminar on Hope Allen's work in the summer of 1984 (coincidentally, the fiftieth anniversary of the identification of the *Book of Margery Kempe*), and I am grateful for the interest and the questions that the seminar generated. At Oxford too I received useful help from Dr. Pamela Gradon, Dr. Anne Hudson and from Mr. David Vaisey, Bodley's Librarian. Much of the book was written at the Warburg Institute, London, and I am grateful to Professor Joseph Trapp, the Director, for the courtesies I enjoyed there. One of the last conversations I had with the late Charles Schmitt, of the Warburg, concerned this book, and there for the last time I had the advantage of his humane learning and balanced but felt judgment.

I am grateful to Georgetown University for a summer grant and for sabbatical leave to work on this book. I am further grateful for useful assistance I have had from friends and colleagues at Georgetown, particularly from Professors Lucy Maddox, Daniel Moshenberg, Patricia O'Connor, Ray Reno, Eusebio Rodrigues, James Slevin, Penn Szittya, Thomas Walsh, and Ms. Marie Currie, Joan Russo, Jean de Silva and the late Mrs. Emilie Dolge, all of the English Department; Professor Elizabeth McKeown of the Theology Department, Professor Emmett Curran, S.J., of the History Department, and Nicholas B. Scheetz of Special Collections. I am very grateful to Professor Paul Ruggiers of Pilgrim Books and the University of Oklahoma, and to his able colleagues, for their careful, helpful and attentive handling of the manuscript. Only my wife's injunction prevents me from saying how much this book actually owes to her.

Georgetown University   J. C. H.
Washington, D.C.

PREFACE

nown intimately by relatively few even in her own lifetime, Hope Emily Allen (1883–1960) is today remembered primarily for her studies of the fourteenth-century English mystic Richard Rolle and for her discovery of the fifteenth-century work the *Book of Margery Kempe*. Her projected second volume of that book never appeared (she is remembered in some circles for that too) but her larger accomplishments were the direction she gave to Middle English studies during its formative period and the contributions she made toward establishing its canon; these achievements have gone largely unobserved, as have her contributions to feminism and to an Anglo-American tradition in literary scholarship. Never surrendering her American sense of things, she found in Britain an enlarged sense of a European culture, a regard for integrity and for feeling, and a number of personal and academic associations, all of which moved her deeply. One language does not mean one culture, but it can imply recognizable correspondences, the influence of a continuum, even a sense of continuity.

In treating Hope Allen's biography, I have focused less on her examination of particular works than on the development of her thought. Oneida, Bryn Mawr, Radcliffe, and Cambridge all left their mark, and I have treated each in its place. I have called the book a study of medieval scholarship and feminism in order to emphasize what I believe to be the two important concerns of her life. Conditioned by British and academic forms as both issues were, Hope's own feminism was exemplary rather than confrontational in practice, but it was profoundly concerned to identify and defend those values, attitudes, and assumptions that medieval women had made their own. These Hope Allen knew to be reflected in some modern values, and she was concerned less with the limitations imposed on medieval women, than with their strength of purpose, spiritual insight, and intellectual influence. Her lifework is steeped in a concern for women's values, and women's identities, and these are constantly recurring themes in her scholarship. Less confrontational than others of her generation, Hope Allen was able to accommodate a markedly successful scholarly career with an ability to work within academic structures, many of which were prejudiced on the issue of gender. In her time the acceptance of women scholars was in its infancy, but Hope's friendships ran deep, and a close academic friend usually became, in time, a friend. I have concerned myself primarily with her British friends – Marietta Pallis, Joan Wake, Dorothy Ellis – though she also maintained close American friends, both in Oneida and in the academic community.

Though in many ways a very private person, Hope Allen moved with unobserved effectiveness to encourage the study of Middle English literary texts that she judged central to the English tradition, particularly those associated with the *Ancrene Riwle*, the title Hope preferred (sometimes *Ancren* without the final -e) to the more primitive *Ancrene Wisse* and the one I have used here, whose current position in the canon is due largely to her efforts. In this undertaking she was sensitive both to the feminist aspects of her work and to the international aspects. She was careful to encourage both American and British scholars, and as a long-term resident of London, she felt keenly the importance of Anglo-American cooperation. That an American woman, working independently and without an academic affiliation, should have accomplished what she did is in itself surprising.

But it has been partly to lessen her formality, partly to make her and her work approachable, that I have claimed the privilege of referring to her, and a very few of her closest friends, by first rather than last name. This was not a habit she encouraged, as the formality which still remains about her professional signature, Hope Emily Allen, makes clear. But it is the personal as well as the professional side of her intellectual life that I am concerned with, and to call her simply Allen recognizes neither. I trust my own esteem is apparent, and will be shared by the reader.

Throughout her life she described herself as an "independent scholar," and by that she meant more than that she never accepted a permanent teaching appointment at a college or university. Her independence, initially enforced by her health, was finally elected, and meant that she was free to go where her research led her, to examine texts that lay outside all but the most recondite syllabus, and to give them and their background closer examination than they had received before.

Though Hope Allen's writing looks all of a piece, it falls in fact into three large, if overlapping, groups: her early work on the *Ancrene Riwle*, her mature study of Richard Rolle, and her examination of the cultural background of the *Book of Margery Kempe*. But contradictions and even ironies are present even in this rather simple grouping. For one thing, she also published numerous short studies on related subjects, and some fiction. For another, her studies on the *Ancrene Riwle* were proceeding at the same time as were those on Rolle. Both the examination of manu-scripts and the search, in recondite sources, for the identities of owners and scribes touched both her studies on Rolle and those on *Ancrene Riwle*, and she herself appears to have ignored any difference in meth-odology, and considered herself a "historical" scholar in each case.

But differences there were. Her work on *Ancrene Riwle* engaged one of the great themes of her scholarly life: the importance of the spirituality of women in the late Middle Ages. It involved not only an identification (Who were the women to whom *Ancrene Riwle* referred?) but also a host of historical, cultural, and interpretative problems not present in her work on Rolle. In fact, after she made her identification in her second really important article much of her subsequent work on *Ancrene Riwle* was concerned with showing the work's importance by locating references to it in other medieval works, the same sort of work, changes having been made, that she had been doing on Rolle.

Her work on Rolle, on the other hand, engaged her in a much more detailed examination than anything she had done before. It was not a matter simply of finding contradictions and impossibilities. Those abounded, as they do in most other medieval manuscripts, but the point was to identify which works were by Richard Rolle. To do so, Hope Allen established four criteria, and that fact alone was a marked advance on her earlier work.

The third phase of her work concerned the *Book of Margery Kempe*. Her study of this extraordinary document caused her to rethink her position on almost every aspect of late-medieval religious life, particularly those that concerned women. She did not live to see her new formulation in print, but its direction is clear from the notes she left behind.

Her home address she invariably gave as "The Mansion House, Ken- wood, Oneida, New York." There she spent her first and last years, and there she often returned, for rest, reflection, and writing, during her years of residence in London and Ann Arbor, Michigan. There the force of past ideals remained like granite, even after the ideals themselves had changed beyond recognition.

John C. Hirsh

Prologue

ONEIDA

Many of the towns in upstate New York appear only loosely attached to the great Republic that lies to the south. They bear names like Rome and Palmyra, Mycenae and Ithaca, and seem to have sprung from Mediterranean settlers, or to have been named at random by a wandering professor of classics. But names, as Hope Allen was to learn, can be deceptive. America has many heartlands, and this is one of them.

By the time Hope Allen was born—on November 12, 1883—the Oneida community that was her home had put its radical past behind it and was attending to business. Yet its origins had not entirely vanished. In March, 1848, John Humphrey Noyes had brought a small group of followers to settle on a farm just outside Oneida, New York. The ideals that moved the group were millenarian: Noyes believed that Christ had already returned to the earth, indeed that he had done so about A.D. 70, when the temple in Jerusalem was destroyed, and that with his return a new order had begun. In preparation for the Final Judgement that would follow, all persons had to achieve and to claim perfection, which meant in practice freedom from sin. Perfection would be best attained, Noyes believed, in what he called a "holy community," where, he had written, "there is no reason why sexual intercourse should be restricted by law, than why eating and drinking should be—and there is as little occasion for shame in one case as in the other." Such pronouncements like this one made in 1837 earned his group few friends except among the committed, and in its first days Oneida seemed as much a refuge as a paradise.

But refuge or no, it was at Oneida that Noyes' plan took hold. Human relationships—and birth—were central to the undertaking, but the approval of a committee, not marriage, was what sanctioned sexual inter-course and the birth of children. This practice Noyes named "complex marriage," complex because the attachment was not for life, nor was it intended to encourage exclusive relationships but was to lead to the creation of good children. "Stirpi-culture" was the word coined to describe these practices. The arrangement was supported by two other Oneida practices, "male continence", a rather primitive form of birth control known as *coitus reservatus*; and "mutual criticism," a practice in which an individual was told publicly by other members of the community what they thought of his attitudes and behavior. It was a practice from which the founder alone was exempt.

For about thirty years the community prospered, helped along by a successful animal trap factory, and during the 1860s the members con-structed the large Victorian Mansion House, which still survives, an outward sign of an apparently successful social dynamic. But by 1878 there were tensions within the community: the second generation was less disposed to accede to the wishes of a committee than the first had been, particularly when Noyes sought to introduce his son as the new head of the community; and these tensions combined with outside attacks, many in newspapers, to bring the perfectionist phase to a close. On June 22, 1879, Noyes suddenly and permanently left the community, settling just across the border in Niagara Falls, Canada. Not long there-after marriage was introduced into the community that he had left behind which he continued to advise by letter, and in September, 1880, by a community vote, Oneida Community was officially and legally broken up, and Oneida Community, Ltd., a joint-stock company that controlled the now-extensive manufacturing, distribution, and sales system, came into being. Hard times lay ahead, but Oneida Community, Ltd., was fortunate in its choice of managers, and the company prospered.

As did its members. Hope Allen's parents, Portia Underhill and Henry C. Allen, Jr., were the sort of people on whom the community had long depended but who have been neglected by scholars focusing attention on Noyes and his well-run printing press. The Allens, as they became, met in the community and parented their first child, Grosvenor Noyes Allen, on January 13, 1874. The birth of the child seems to have increased their love, so much so that it was reckoned a special attachment, and the two were directed to separate. They did so, but their love remained, and after the breakup of the community they married.

In November, 1883, the couple gave birth to their second and last child, Hope Emily Allen. Later in life Hope attributed much of her interest in medieval religion to her parents' attachment to Oneida, which she thought sprang from their desire to escape the religious legalisms of their childhood. But while her father's family had been connected to Oneida since 1850, her mother's family had not and after their daughter's conversion in 1865, achieved in part by her unreturned love for one of John Humphrey Noyes' younger brothers, severed all connection with her. Hope's family was English on both sides, but her mother's English cousins included Evelyn Underhill, an authority on mysticism who in 1934 made possible Hope's discovery of the *Book of Margery Kempe*. But Hope remembered too that her mother's family was Episcopalian and so brought a degree of theological sophistication into her childhood.

Hope grew up in what appears to have been a protective and supportive environment. Often sickly (she was thought in childhood to be tubercular) she was watched carefully and spent her summers at the Mansion House or in the Adirondacks. She early acquired an interest in genealogy, and her family has a carefully kept book of the Allen descent, which Hope prepared during her school days, and gives the first hint of the exactness of mind and focus on individual persons that would inform her mature work.

Her school was the Niagara Falls Collegiate Institution, in Canada, where her grades were among the highest in her class, and where her best subjects were Latin, ancient history, French, algebra, and geometry. A schoolgirl diary of 1899–1900 records her early interests: a delight in the countryside and an interest in her Puritan forebears, in writing stories, in friends. The diary tells too of a crisis that troubled her sixteenth year, when she decided not to attended college as she had hoped and her family had expected but to become a writer instead. She would support herself with jobs, for example, in the public library. She loved Oneida and the countryside around and was in no hurry to leave.

It was not to be. No one insisted, but all advised against. Her admired brother, Grosvenor, who declined to fall in with her plans, was, unknown to Hope, helping defeat a strike in the Canadian factories by importing workers from New York: "silly and senseless" were the words he used to describe her refusal. Her father insisted that the family finances were stronger than Hope had thought. Her mother urged her to attend college. Even the close girlhood friend to whom Hope addressed—and lent—her diary asked "do you fully understand what you are giving up?" In the end Hope agreed, and from all appearances her enthusiasm for college returned. The reasons for the choice are not clear, but Hope applied to, and was accepted by, Bryn Mawr College, just outside Philadelphia, for the class of 1905. The Oneida traditions of respecting quality, of setting aside the usual limitations of a woman's sphere, and of getting away from the community, if only for a time, worked to her advantage, and she enrolled in an institution that would claim her affections, broaden her outlook, and provide a direction that she would maintain for the rest of her working life.

BRYN MAWR AND RADCLIFFE

Apart from Oneida, the most important influence on Hope's work and feminism was her education, first at Bryn Mawr, from which she graduated in 1905, subsequently at Radcliffe College. But the effects of these two institutions, as I shall show in this chapter, were very different.

In 1900, Bryn Mawr was still a relatively young institution, as were most women's colleges in the United States. Founded in 1885 by Dr. Joseph Wright Taylor, a Quaker physician from Burlington, New Jersey, it had, since 1894, been headed by one of the most remarkable women in America, President M. Carey Thomas ("P. T." among the students), who had very distinct ideas about what a woman's education should be. Bryn Mawr already had several traditions by the time Hope Allen enrolled, a number of which were Quaker.

Dr. Taylor had resolved to found the college in the 1870s when he saw, in part because of the changed society which emerged from the Civil War, that women would be required to assume a greater role than that hitherto allowed them. He believed that teaching, long within their sphere, would increase in importance and that Quaker women, for whom Dr. Taylor primarily intended his college, would need better education than that currently available. In 1877 he endowed the college in his will. After he died in 1880 another physician, Dr. James E. Rhoads, became the first president. In a letter read to the trustees after his death, Dr. Taylor urged that decorum in dress, outdoor exercise, and "a very high degree of refinement of heart, mind and manners" should prevail. More academic matters, like a faculty and a curriculum, he left to others, but he took a practical interest in selecting the site, a rise of ground about fourteen miles from Philadelphia, and in planning the construction of the buildings. But it was the academic development of the college that would make it famous. From the first it aimed at providing both a good undergraduate and a good graduate education, and from early on offered master's and doctoral degrees in several disciplines. This practice carried with it certain conditions: The faculty could not be restricted to Quakers or to women. Hard work would be required of all. Bryn Mawr students, unlike their contemporaries at Mount Holyoke, for example, would not do housework, nor would "practical courses in home economy" be included in the curriculum. The college was for the talented (entrance standards were high), and the ambitious (the work was demanding). It was not, however, socially sensitive, and did nothing to encourage applications from black students.

However dedicated to the cause of women's education Bryn Mawr would become (it remains a women's college on the undergraduate level to this day), it attracted to its faculty both men and women of unusually high quality. Thus, however pastoral its appearance, it gave access to a wider world of learning than any of its students had yet encountered. In class, professors made easy and frequent reference to colleagues in other universities, in other nations. In courses on literature manuscripts were cited to alert attentive students to the great libraries of Europe. During the period Hope was attending, a new library, Rockefeller Hall, was under construction and would be finished in 1904, the year before her graduation. Connection with Philadelphia, then as now by train, was easy and convenient, and Bryn Mawr broke with tradition by allowing its students to smoke. Taken as a whole, the college can only have been a liberating experience for the new student from Oneida.

Not only did the college offer a wide variety of opportunity; its president offered strong direction. Born in 1857, Dr. M. (for Martha) Carey Thomas came from a Baltimore Quaker family that had been involved in the founding of Bryn Mawr. Educated in Quaker schools, she graduated from Cornell with honors in 1877. Determined to continue her education, she entered, with special permission because her father was on the Board of Trustees, Johns Hopkins University, but was forbidden to attend classes, though it may have been intimated to her that she might listen to lectures from behind a curtain! Such practices, common enough in graduate education for women for some decades, were as insulting as they were stupid, and Carey Thomas decided to study in Germany, where, she had come to believe, true education could be had. She intended to go with a close friend, Mamie Gwinn, whom she had known since childhood, and whom she credited with introducing her to the book that had formulated her view of society, William Godwin's *Enquiry Concerning Political Justice.* Her father, influenced by disapproving friends, initially forbade her voyage, but she attended to her supportive mother's advice, "Thee must cry thyself to Germany," and persevered.

The choice of Germany over England was deliberate. Carey Thomas believed that English scholarship, even in her field, English literature, was amateurish and impressionistic. Rigor, she thought, belonged to Germany. Leipzig refused her entry because of her gender, nor would her second choice, Göttingen, admit her. But the University of Zurich would, and so she went to Switzerland. There she continued a topic begun during a brief period of study in Germany, a philological examination of the fourteenth-century English romance *Sir Gawain and the Green Knight,* but added to it, as her Swiss program required, an introduction, in German, to Swinburne. Her final examination consisted in three days of written examinations on Germanic philology and a three-hour oral examination, in German, on Anglo-Saxon philology and English historical grammar; German, Gothic and Old High German; Middle High German and German literature; and, almost as an afterthought, on the development of English literature. In the end she was awarded the university's highest distinction, the rarely used summa cum laude; her doctorate was awarded in November, 1882.

Returning to America after further travel in Europe, Carey Thomas was in time to assist with the opening of Bryn Mawr, where both her father and an uncle were trustees, for whose presidency she somewhat precipitously (and presumptuously, according to some of the less imaginative trustees) applied. But she had not badly misjudged her political strength and emerged as both dean and professor of English. Hers was the only professorial appointment the new college made.

In Bryn Mawr's first days the German emphasis was pronounced. Four of the first five associate professors had done graduate work in Germany, as had two of the three associates, though they had no previous teaching experience. The third instructor was Woodrow Wilson, the future American president, who took his doctorate from Johns Hopkins in 1886 while he was still teaching at Bryn Mawr, and who came highly recommended. But his association with Carey Thomas was not close, and she resented the way he went over her head to tender an early resignation to the board of trustees.

Like many other able administrators, Carey Thomas did not relish opposition. By the time she became president in 1894, she was already a powerful force on campus, and any decision of importance was referred to her. Her personality often tended to dominate academic matters, and she waged a number of battles with professors she believed opposed her, sometimes with unpleasantly public recriminations, but at least she had a motivating reason for her attitudes: the cause of women. In 1899, two years before Hope Allen arrived on campus, she made headlines by attacking Charles W. Eliot, president of Harvard: "In President Eliot's otherwise luminous intelligence," she wrote, "women's education is [a] dark spot."

She was keenly aware of the competitive aspect of education and opposed special legislation for women, whom she believed the equal or better of men. Under her the true Bryn Mawr "type" was neither plodding nor lazy; she was ambitious and would prosper, usually in one or other of the professions. If she was a true scholar, she would be unlikely to marry, since she had to enjoy the freedom to put her work before anything else. Foreign travel and graduate education were essentials. "Whatever we may think of women's rights to gain a livelihood in any given occupation," she wrote in a 1901 article in the *Educational Review*, "we must all agree that, if they are to compete successfully with men engaged in this same occupation, they must receive as thorough and prolonged a preparation for it as men." In one commencement address she paid particular attention to graduate students, and to those going on to graduate and to foreign universities. Armed with her Bryn Mawr education, such a student would have gained the confidence Carey Thomas believed to be part of the price that success required, a confidence based on expert training and hard work. In this way Bryn Mawr would remake attitudes not only towards women's education, but also toward women.

Powerful and committed, Carey Thomas left a marked impression on all she met, and particularly on Bryn Mawr students. "I have forgotten everything I learned at Bryn Mawr," one student wrote to her years later, "but I still see you standing in chapel and telling us to believe in women."

Believe in women Carey Thomas did, and yet one other aspect of her personality, her close attachment to two women scholars, did not escape attention. I have already mentioned Mamie Gwinn, the girlhood friend with whom she traveled to Germany and Switzerland, and who became an instructor in the English Department. In 1904, after many tribulations, Mamie Gwinn eloped with Alfred Hodder, a former Bryn Mawr English teacher, an event that became the subject of *Fernhurst*, a minor novel by Gertrude Stein. Mamie Gwinn's place was thereafter taken by another close school friend, Mary Garrett, who moved into Carey Thomas's home, the Deanery, in 1903, remaining there until her death in 1915. Carey Thomas's relationship with both women was one of mutual support, which appears not to have been physical. Still it is unlikely that the closeness of the relationships would have escaped the more perceptive students.

It may be worth asking, even before we turn to Hope Allen's career at Bryn Mawr, how much of the Bryn Mawr attitude towards women and scholarship she absorbed. The answer appears to be much of it. Whether for reasons of doctrine, health, or coincidence, Hope Allen never married, and she continued her graduate studies first at Radcliffe and then at Cambridge University. She became in time an able and productive scholar. In this she was no doubt influenced by the standard set for her, a standard that would have been congenial to a disposition formed in part by the selective and rigorous requirements of Oneida. She kept the level of scholarship and deportment expected of a Bryn Mawr graduate, remaining throughout her life concerned with the role of women, and in her scholarship she was equal to, or better than, her male colleagues.

Teacher-student relationships are complex, and though Hope Allen was attracted to much of what Carey Thomas taught, she rejected some of it. For one thing, she did not pursue the same course of study Carey Thomas had followed. Both women chose medieval English literature as their area of specialization, but where Carey Thomas's approach was that of Germanic philology, Hope Allen's was, as she came to describe it, historical. Turning aside from, but perhaps not rejecting, the earlier philological tradition, she focused on the texts, authors, and owners of manuscripts that were not then much studied, and did so in the humane belief that these aspects would clarify the conditions of which the texts spoke. Her choice of England rather than Germany (both were possible in 1910) had an ideological as well as a cultural aspect. She wanted to address her texts in the nation of their composition, the nation, more than incidentally, from which her own ancestors had come.

Further, her commitment to what Carey Thomas called "the cause of women" was intellectual before it was anything else. She listed herself as an "independent scholar" throughout her working life. Close friendships, primarily with other women scholars but also with men, she was to have, and these supported rather than inhibited her work. Personal power in the academy had little interest for her, except when it directly touched upon her work, and this was an attitude Carey Thomas could hardly have understood. It was as though, for reasons of temperment, belief, or tact, she consciously turned away from the public forum Carey Thomas approved and sought instead to identify the intellectual, moral, and historical foundations for the kinds of feminism that most moved her. This was a choice that began at Bryn Mawr when she began to turn from creative to scholarly writing, but it is difficult not to see in it an exception being taken both to the style and to some of the substance of what Carey Thomas taught. Yet there can be no doubt that her years at Bryn Mawr were the most satisfying and rewarding academic experience of her life.

At Bryn Mawr, Hope first encountered the Middle Ages in depth. It may only have been the requirements of the curriculum that placed her, in her first semester, in a medieval history class, but she passed it, and her Freshman course in English literature, with honors. In her second year she added classes in Shakespeare and in elocution and began her first year of essay work, which was to prove one of her greatest strengths. That year she also took up French literature and modern history. Thus by June, 1903, the end of her second year, she had already established something of a presence at Bryn Mawr. Her grades, always high, had placed her among the ablest of her contemporaries, and she was in a particularly good class. In the end she finished fifth, but with such high grades that in another year she would have stood even higher.

Apart from her academic record, there is one other important indication of her development during this period. Her family correspondence, particularly her letters to her mother, but also those to her father and brother, show, somewhat guardedly, what was on her mind (these letters are today preserved in Syracuse University Library). Then as now, undergraduate letters home were not entirely candid, and Hope's are no exception to that rule, but at a number of places they depart from the usual assurances to give an insight into what she was thinking. Through-out this period it was she, not her family, who must have seemed fixed. Her mother now lived much of the time in Niagara Falls and wintered in Phoenix, Arizona, for her health; her father went frequently to Canada on business; and her much-loved brother Grosvenor, ten years older than Hope, was in the Oneida factory in Chicago, though he was later recalled to Oneida when his work, designing the high-quality tableware which was to replace animal traps as the maker of Oneida's fortunes, made him more valuable at the home office.

But Hope reveled in Bryn Mawr. In her second year she wrote in a Valentine's Day letter to Grosvenor:

> They have started an English Club which you may be interested in hearing about. It is for the purpose of creating a literary set, stimulating literary ambitions, etc. It is just organized this week—I have heard about it for a long time from Maud Temple, whom I know well. She, perhaps I have told you of her, writes as well I suppose as any person in College if not better: she is of course a member, the only junior (she is to be the editor in chief of The Lantern next year—and will of course be prize Essayist). The Club is formed more or less on the lines of the Radcliffe Club—Its membership is restricted to 8, and for membership one high credit on a semester's work in essay work, or two credits are necessary for application—but eligibility won't mean acceptance . . . this of course makes the club extremely exclusive.

Just a week before, on February 7, 1903, she had written to her mother about recent events, and one in particular. Her examinations were just over, and, anticipating a concern for her health, she insisted: "I wasn't at all worn out and enjoyed my examinations almost—though of course I am glad to have them over," before turning to an even more recent event.

> Last night I went to a lecture by an English woman, a Mrs Witherington, on the New English Education Bill. The speaker was typically not Ameri-can—she wore the usual ill-fitting clothes English women seem to, and had very fresh color and an English face—Her lecture made me hope that there were Americans like her—there was nothing precious about it—it was only a bare statement of the conditions of English education under the New Education Bill, prefaced for clearness by a study of the conditions that have formerly prevailed there—Mrs. Witherington made the apology to her speech, that she feared she was going to introduce us to a confused and

chaotic subject to which any sort of comprehension was only possible by means of much detail and bare information. She had no notes whatsoever, and in point of clearness and closed iron-bound sequences, her speech was one of the most remarkable things I ever heard—I think she is about the most clear-headed woman I have every seen. Her language was perfectly adequate always, she never stuttered or paused for the word and she made her subject so clear, and with that so interesting, that I think I absorbed more information from her lecture than from almost any I ever heard. It is such a pleasure to hear a perfectly clearheaded person.

However self-conscious her language, Hope's pleasure in Mrs. Witherington's clarity, but also in Mrs. Witherington herself, shines through. It may not be too much to see in her wish that there may be Americans like her the beginning of Hope's attraction to Britain.

During her last two years at Bryn Mawr, Hope's thinking appears to have hardened. She still intended to pursue a career as a writer, but it was during this time too that her interest in medieval literature took root and developed. Her formal studies now became increasingly useful to an aspiring medievalist. Junior year saw a concentration in Greek, with Homer, whom she particularly enjoyed, followed by Plato and Euripides. Her work in English composition ran concurrently, as did work in major English critics and in Old English grammar. But the most important course she took in her junior year was in medieval romances, though her initial reaction was not admiring. Writing to her mother on October 22, 1903, she remarked her interest in Burke, "both the style and the man," and went on:

> I am also having a course in Middle English Romances that is nice especially as it isn't much work. These old romances are charming reading I think. I enjoy Homer very much too, and hope to get soon so that I can read Greek aloud well.

But by the end of the semester the romances had won her over. On December 15 she remarked that in her English course

> We read the most charming old Middle English Romances, just as our forefathers read them about 1100.

But other influences were at work too, one of which clearly foreshadowed her future pursuits. Indeed, the single most important intellec-

12

tual influence of Hope's junior year was a lecture delivered by Mary Logan Smith Berenson, Bernhard Berenson's wife, in February, 1904. Mary Berenson, a cousin of Carey Thomas, came from an affluent Quaker family, and took an early interest in Bryn Mawr. A remarkable woman by any standard, her contribution to art history, located in her husband's notebooks and publications, is only now being understood. She at once attracted Hope Allen.

Hope attended the lecture, on which she reported in the March 1904, issue of *Tipyn o Bob*, the monthly student literary magazine of which she soon became editor. Her report, "Mrs. Berenson's Lecture on the New Art Criticism," anticipated to an astonishing degree methods, ideas, and approaches that she adopted in subsequent decades, as she carefully formulated and decided attributions of works to the fourteenth-century English mystic Richard Rolle.

She began her article by citing Mrs. Berenson's closing remarks about the qualities in a painting which are impossible to "pass on" but which one can only experience. What the Berensons sought to do, she wrote, was rather "to introduce critical method" into attribution, rejecting "the frequently careless statements of contemporaries," since "accuracy in naming, Mrs. Berenson believes, is really extremely to be desired." She gave reasons: good paintings are likely to be passed over if they are misidentified, just as inferior ones are likely to be praised; but it was the call to accuracy to which Hope Allen, her work on Oneida genealogies not far behind her, responded.

Mary Berenson told the students that her work had been based on that of Giovanni Morelli, who had noticed that certain details in an artist's oeuvre, the ear, for example, or the hair, remained constant and provided the best possible clue to the identity of the artist. "There is always some tell-tale mark of the author," Hope triumphantly wrote, quoting Berenson in insisting that "the tests must be entirely mechanical, – documentary and internal." Such identifications led to "the contemplation of what is really masterly" so as "to grasp the beauty of a great picture," which will influence "one's outlook on life." It is not too much to say that the approach Mary Berenson described anticipated in some detail Hope's later treatment of Richard Rolle's canon.

Other literary efforts that Hope published about this time were less interesting. The month before she had reported on Professor Barrett

Wendell's lecture on Puritanism ("that ever-present type of humanity"), one of her own favorite topics; and the following month she wrote on gift books of the 1840s, a small collection of which she owned, and which she called "some relics of popular taste." These productions, together with some light verse, put her in line for the editorship in the fall of her senior year. *Typyn o Bob* was an interesting choice. Less formal and a good deal more lively than the more majestic student literary magazine, *The Lantern*, for which she also wrote, *Tipyn* engaged a range of campus issues but also published fiction and light verse and generally sought to amuse, not edify.

Thus her senior year was particularly active and demanding. She continued her Greek with Demosthenes, Aristophanes, Sophocles, and Thucydides and studied minor English poets, descriptive writing, general philosophy and psychology. In her last semester she also elected a course in early English narrative writing, clearly by this time consolidating her graduate career. In December she took the two oral examinations required of graduating seniors, passing the French exam but not the German. She failed the German again in March, an irony for the future scholar of German mystics, but passed it in April. In fact her campus responsibilities were many, and it is not clear how much time she had to devote to her German. The October issue of *Tipyn o Bob* carries an unsigned editorial that was already vintage Hope Allen. Treating the Quaker origins of Bryn Mawr, she wrote as one "not born into the Community of Friends" who can speak from only "scanty knowledge" about "the peculiar turn of the Quaker mind." she noted that

> We remember that the early Quakers denied themselves most sensuous indulgence: they set their faces against many hide-bound conventions of society: and they distrusted the material things of the world even when symbolic of the immaterial, inasmuch as they made their devotions without ritual or outward sign. So theirs were ideals of simplicity of living and sobriety of intellect. They showed forth in their ideals a rare chastity of mind.

It was about this time that Hope was turning from the Christianity in which she had been reared in Oneida, to the unassertive agnosticism that she maintained throughout her life. Part of the attraction of Bryn Mawr was that it provided an alternative to the more enthusiastic traditions of

Oneida while continuing to attach a degree of respect to that bedrock of Oneida, the individual conscience. She met, in the course of her last years at Bryn Mawr, many of the more important Quakers in Philadelphia and came to attribute some part of her interest in mystics to her meeting with Rufus Jones, the Bryn Mawr trustee who taught at the University of Pennsylvania, and whose books she continued to acknowledge as late as 1940. But even Quaker influences rested uneasily on her determined intelligence, and before long she set aside all but the most conventional religious connections.

A related alliance that came into question about this time was that with Oneida. Throughout her years at Bryn Mawr she listed her address as "Niagara Falls Center, Ontario, Canada." The address was not inaccurate, since she spent most of her summers there with her mother; but she equally identified herself with New York State: a piece in the November, 1904, *Tipyn o Bob* described the lakeside areas of New York, and it is probable that in her youth she had mixed feelings about her Oneida heritage. Privately she knew where her roots were. A letter to her mother of February 24, 1903, referred to Goldwin Smith's essay "American Socialism of the Oneida Community" as giving "us" the "benefit of the scientific method of analysis without partisanship." But she avoided writing about Oneida itself, which had still, in some polite circles, a mixed reputation.

If Mary Berenson's lecture was the high point of her junior year, it was Henry James's lectures during his visit to America in 1905 that distinguished her senior year. James came twice to Bryn Mawr, once to lecture on Balzac, and once to give the commencement address, and each time Hope Allen recorded the substance of what he said, the first address in the February, 1905, issue of *Tipyn o Bob*, the second time in the yearbook. In February too, as president of the English Club, she was allowed to meet the great man, who was at his most engaging, and she gave a description of the event, a meeting with the student presidents of campus organizations, in a letter to her mother dated February 8, 1905:

> He is astonishingly genial and humorous, and kept us all laughing. He was much amused by the many presidents, and declared he never saw such a 'presidential gathering' and he hailed each girl with the query 'are you a president? Don't tell me that you aren't'!—when the president of the Athletic Assoc. came last, he cried 'Good, Good, Good,' when assured

that this was another, . . . he gave her such an athletic hand grasp that he said over and over again that he should never get over it.

But it was the address on Balzac that most claimed Hope's attention. In her account in *Tipyn o Bob*, she noted not only James's "intellectual keenness" but also his "earnestness and likableness, which we had not expected." The lecture, subsequently published, turned on an apprecia- tion of the French author's "closeness and weight," which stood against "the cheap and easy" of modern taste. "One must take his work *en masse*," James insisted, since, however large the canon, it is by canon alone that any author must stand or fail. Balzac appealed to James because, as Hope recorded: "he does not concern himself with his own image of life, but with the states and feelings of others." Balzac's life James acknowledged to have been "one of the great puzzles of literary history." He had died at fifty, "worn out with thought, and work, and passion," but for the twenty years before his death he had created a picture of life in France "bristling with information, facts, figures; a rank tropical forest of detail and specific information, but with the strong wind of genius circulating through it." In Balzac's life, Hope wrote, the lecturer had insisted that

> experience must have come vicariously. We, too, live vicariously, said Mr. James. Our imagination opens dusty passages for us in life, but they are short, we come to a gate, the walls are without resonance, and the candles go out. Balzac's luxury is in the extraordinary number and length of his passages, corridors and labyrinths in which he can lose himself.

Balzac's "sign," James believed, was "quantity and intensity," and, in a final remark that must have gone home, he added that "nothing counts but excellence; nothing exists for estimation but the superlative of its particu- lar kind."

Like Mary Berenson, Henry James registered deeply with Hope. Her account of his performance, which also gave attention to his "variety of amplification and luxuriance of phase," anticipates her own later work, not methodologically but thematically, particularly in its attention to canon and to the necessity of entering into the "states and feelings of others." No doubt James' concern for biography was already Hope's too, the Oneida genealogies having had their effect. But here was a larger consideration: that facts required "the strong wind of genius" to give them meaning. If like Balzac (and like James) the scholar lived, at least in part, vicariously, he or she lived still by the imagination, sympathetic to the excellence of others, and so making his or her own. Much of this Hope was to reformulate and refine over the years, but in her account of James's lecture much of her later creed exists in embryo.

The remainder of her senior year appears to have passed without incident, her German oral apart. As president of the English Club, Hope was responsible for bringing a speaker to campus, and she first approached Professor Horace Howard Furness Jr., of Harvard, who declined. She then approached President LeBaron R. Briggs of Radcliffe College, who, urged by President Carey Thomas, accepted. The lecture, given in January, 1905, was on the poetry of John Donne, an avant garde topic for its day, but its importance for Hope was less the substance than the fact that the speaker came from Radcliffe and evidently esteemed Bryn Mawr. After a final year of graduate study at Bryn Mawr, she would go to Radcliffe herself.

Her last months as an undergraduate were distinguished in other ways. She continued to write, and some of her college themes, essays required in courses, were printed, as the best ones traditionally were, in *The Lantern*. "A Portrait,' one of her best, alludes to "my own Puritan ancestors," whom she credited with "stern consistency" a quality she continued to admire. At her graduation James appeared again, this time as commencement speaker, but his address, which Hope reported for the yearbook, was something of a disappointment, and there is a note of resentment against his topic, "Securities and Serenities." "He did not," Hope observed, "bring a new gospel to the barbarians," though not everyone agreed with his analysis, which anyway his audience had heard before, perhaps too often. "Speaking is the very life of our life," Hope paraphrased without enthusiasm. "Beautiful speaking is the index of much else that is beautiful. It makes a part of a great and significant whole, of the great general habit of good breeding." This was not a theme Hope could warm to, and it is instructive that she gave it less space than she did an account, in the same yearbook, of the junior-senior supper.

Yet in other ways her graduation had been a great success. She was awarded a $200 graduate fellowship in English, and graduated fifth among "The Ten," the students with the highest academic averages. In early May she was awarded the George W. Childs Essay Prize, given each year, she informed her mother on May 3, "to a Senior whom the essay department pronounces to do the best writing. It is a gold watch given at commencement." She had thus established herself as the most promising, as well as the most accomplished, student of English literature in her class, and she knew it. This habit of mind she maintained through-out her life, which academically was about to begin.

Hope spent her final year at Bryn Mawr as a graduate student. At the end of it she was awarded an M.A., which was to prove her final degree, though the distinction was rather more impressive than it has since become. During this time she continued to pursue her career as a writer. *The Lantern* for 1906 carried what was in some ways her most ambitious short story to date, "Haldimand," in which the protagonist, Mary Copley, of "plain English stock," returns to Haldimand, "a forlorn little town" after having been to Europe, where she "never expected to go" to find her school friend, Ned Parnell "ready to cut loose from things." She avoids Ned after their first meeting, and refuses to write to him but registers "a shock" at his subsequent declaration: "'I've got to make a dash and be independent somehow. I'm going to Schenectady.'" At the end of the story she sets off to visit a school friend in Toronto, knowing that Ned will be gone on her return. She leaves with "sorrow and hope in plenty, but no fear."

The fellowships she received were very useful, but she knew that she would continue to require assistance from Oneida. When she took up graduate work, she did so in two fields, English literature and Greek. Her curriculum was approved by President Carey Thomas, as the custom was, and included a major seminar in Middle English taught by Carleton Brown and courses in Plato and Lucian. Her work with the English Journal Club continued into her graduate career at Bryn Mawr and allowed her to continue with creative work at a time when her scholarly powers were likewise developing. If she had any mixed feelings about continuing with medieval English, they may have been dispelled by Carleton Brown, with whom, however, she would always preserve a certain distance. In 1906 Brown was at the beginning of what was to prove a very distinguished career, one that was, as Hope's was to be, intimately associated with the examination of medieval manuscripts. He had only recently arrived at Bryn Mawr after a two-year instructorship at Harvard, where in 1903 he had taken his Ph.D., a late entrant into academic life. Born in 1869, he had attended Carleton College, where he had taken his first degree at eighteen. After two years of editing a biweekly newspaper in Colorado, he had, in 1890, entered Andover Seminary, and in 1894 was ordained a Unitarian minister. For the next six years he served as a minister, first in Saint Cloud, Minnesota, and after 1897 in Helena, Montana. It was from Helena that, in 1900, he entered Harvard. In later years he entertained friends with stories of his days in the early American West.

During the year Hope graduated, Brown's article "The Author of *Pearl* Considered in the Light of His Theological Opinions" appeared in *PMLA* and showed an individual mind at work at the heart of a complex religious poem. He became best known for three anthologies of medieval religious lyrics, and later for *The Index of Middle English Verse*, which he published with Rossell Hope Robbins. Professionally, his most important contribution was his work with the Modern Language Association of America, which is still the most important professional body for scholars of English and modern languages.

His relationship with his most distinguished student was correct and formal, thought not really warm. Following the more formal conventions of the period, they never used first-names, though Brown congratulated her on her academic distinctions and, as editor, regularly accepted her articles for *PMLA*. Hope's last major study appeared in his 1940 festschrift. There is ample evidence of his support throughout her working life. It was Brown who introduced her both to Richard Rolle, and to the *Ancrene Riwle*, the two great and continuing interests of her academic life, and who first directed her studies of medieval literature. It may have been he who pointed out to her George Perry's edition of Rolle, published for the Early English Text Society in 1866, which included a note requesting information about manuscripts for a "perfect list of the English writings of Richard Rolle" and which the committee of the EETS was seeking to establish.

Between her last year at Bryn Mawr and her first at Radcliffe, she spent a year with her family in Oneida. The reason for this hiatus is revealed in a letter written on April 6, 1944 (now in Oxford), to Dr. Mabel Day, a future colleague. In it Hope reported that she had recently found a letter her doctor had written to her father in 1907 (which I have not traced), stating that, in his opinion, Hope had contracted tuberculosis. Writing in 1944, Hope's only remark was "what an interesting 35 years I have had since then," which suggests that the prognosis of 1907 was not optimistic; but tuberculosis was serious business, and it says much about Hope's firmness of purpose that she was able to enroll at Radcliffe the next year.

She arrived at Radcliffe with her interest in Richard Rolle already well advanced and that in the *Ancrene Riwle* begun. In her first year she took George Lyman Kittredge's course in Shakespeare, George Baker's in English Drama, and Edward Sheldon's in Old French. She also took two courses with William Henry Schofield, who had become her academic adviser, one in fourteenth- and fifteenth-century English literature, and a course simply listed as research, which probably was to allow her to continue her work on Richard Rolle. In addition she took two courses at Harvard University, William Allen Nelson's comparative medieval literature, and a medieval English course with F. N. Robinson. Her second year continued this program, though with a slightly modified course load, occasioned by a recurrence of ill health. But in 1909–10 she took two more courses with Schofield, her adviser, who had evidently become something of a supporter, again one in fourteenth- and fifteenth-century English and continental literature, and another research course. She also studied Gothic philology and took another Harvard course, Charles Homer Haskins' famous class in medieval history.

Radcliffe was a very mixed experience for her. Her letters to Dean Mary Coes express a sincere pleasure in the place, and she was never slow to list her conenction with Radcliffe in later years. But there are indications that her connections with Harvard, and with those aspects of Radcliffe connected with Harvard, were less happy. At the time Hope Allen was a student there, Radcliffe had no faculty of its own, and lectures to its students were repeated from those given at Harvard, sometimes by the professor himself, but more often by an assistant. The practice was condescending, demeaning and offensive to many Radcliffe students like Hope Allen, though practical and historical reasons for its continuation could always be trotted out. Evidence of Hope's reaction is preserved in a carbon copy (now in Oxford), of a letter she wrote in 1928 to the *London Times* on the subject of women's education, specifically whether Cambridge University should award degrees to women, as Oxford had done since 1920 (in the event, Cambridge did not do so until 1948).

The letter concerns a debate that lapped over onto several matters, but seems to have begun when medical authorities wished to eject certain women medical students, admitted during the difficult days of World War I, from London hospitals, an exercise that brought out the worst attitudes of the British medical profession. The story broke on March 20, 1928, and at once encountered protest, which was answered on March 22 by Dr. James Purves-Stewart, senior physician at Westminster Hospital.

> It may be that some teachers (especially women teachers) can give adequate and detailed instruction to a mixed class of young women and young men on sexual diseases and abnormalities without a shadow of embarrassment either to the teacher or to any member of the audience. There is even a school of thought which prefers these subjects to be discussed open and unashamed. But I confess that were I an undergraduate again (I hope I shall always remain a medical student) I should prefer to seek such knowledge at the feet of a teacher of my own sex, someone whom I could freely cross-examine upon the many obscurities which are bound to arise . . . a large proportion of women students, usually the most brilliant and attractive, promptly marry, and . . . women doctors who take up the career of matrimony rarely persevere with that of medical practice. . . . The admission of women students to men's undergraduate classes is being abandoned, not from any hostility to women, but in the interest of men and women students alike.

The unctuous clichés of Dr. Purves-Stewart's letter were particularly damaging since they reflected a debate on women's education generally, which was being carried on concurrently. About the same time he wrote, various *Times* correspondents had taken up the admission of women to degrees at Cambridge. The American example was adduced as a possible model, and it was to this point that Hope wrote, but no doubt with the medical issue in mind too. Identifying herself as a "research scholar . . . both at Radcliffe and at Newnham," she insisted that "the precedent of Radcliffe does not fit the case of Newnham and Girton. To make it do so it would be necessary to reorganize the Cambridge women's colleges root and branch, and exclude the women from lectures and examinations to which they have been admitted for more than a generation." The position of women at Radcliffe varies with different departments, she explained, and there are some (generally those most rarely chosen) where women are allowed to enter Harvard courses. In the majority of cases however the Harvard lectures are repeated at Radcliffe for the women – often by subordinate instructors, since obviously there is a limit to the number of repetitions that an already over-burdened American professor can undertake, however generously disposed towards the cause of women's education. In my own department while a research student at Radcliffe there was not a single course graduate or undergraduate open to women, and the few courses which the most distinguished lecturers could spare the time for at Radcliffe had to be utilized for students of various degrees of advancement – with obvious loss to the graduate students. The women in my department received great individual generosity from the Harvard faculty, but the system put us in a most tantalizing situation. . . . I recall how after being forbidden many unique opportunitites (and granted some) at Cambridge, America, I came to Cambridge, England, and found women enjoying, as it seemed to me, the liberal tolerance which has been so often the peculiar generosity of the English. At that time we were told that degrees could not be granted to women because they carried votes with them. Now that women suffrage has come the refusal of the degrees at Cambridge becomes purely illogical.

It may be that her feelings about the rules at Radcliffe lessened with time, but it is easy to see how strongly she felt about the gender bias she had encountered. The "distinguished lecturers" whose courses disadvantaged women graduate students no doubt included both Kittredge and Baker, just as the personal kindness she acknowledges came primarily from Schofield. But her irritation with condescension is hardly disguised in the letter, and it may have been for that reason, among others, that it never appeared in print. Still, it makes very clear how she felt about some of the practices she encountered at Radcliffe, so different, as I have shown, from what she had known at Bryn Mawr, and suggests too why she struck out as she did for advanced study in England, as I shall show in the following chapter.

2

TO ENGLAND

ope's academic work was deeply indebted to what she would learn in Britain. Expecting in 1910 simply to examine manuscripts, she found much more, both in the way of academic direction and in professional and personal friendships. In this chapter I shall examine each of these influences.

Hope made her first trip to England in 1910, when she went with her mother on a fellowship from the American Association of Collegiate Alumnae, supplemented by a donation from an aunt, to study Richard Rolle manuscripts. On April 16 of that year Carleton Brown wrote to congratulate her on the award ("it is an honor well bestowed") and to report his own continuing interest in Rolle ("I think few persons will be more directly interested in your conclusions"). Her quest for Rolle manuscipts was connected to her thesis topic, "A Study of the Canon of Richard Rolle of Hampole," but getting approval evidently cost her some effort. A letter from a friend dated November 9, 1909, expostulates: "If only Mr. Kittredge will approve your Richard Rolle paper for the dissertation! It would save you so much." The paper in question was probably Hope's study of the late Middle English poem *The Prick of Conscience*, in which she disproved Rolle's authorship, but in point of fact her relationship with George Lyman Kittredge was complicated and initially, at least, seems not to have gone particularly well. Kittredge's practice was to leave graduate students, even beginning ones, to sink or swim, and he was not greatly concerned with which course they followed. By 1908 he had been twelve years in his chair, to which he had been appointed at the age of thirty-six, and was by any standard a formidable academic. In time he and Hope established a working relationship, he even expressed an interest in the Oneida Indian stories she had collected, one of which, years later, she sent him for publication in one of his many studies of American culture. Although he never used the story, his interest gener-ally pleased Hope, and their relationship gradually improved. In the end, as chairman of the English Department, he approved her thesis topic, and assisted her in her desire to study in Britain. But it is possible to believe that the great man did little to mitigate the condescension she experi-enced in Cambridge.

Once she had obtained her fellowship, Hope approached Newnham College, Cambridge, for permission to enroll for one term to study English literature, noting in her application that she was working toward a Ph.D. at Radcliffe. On April 28, 1910, the general committee of Newnham College approved her admission "if there is room." She was attached to Anna Paues, Newnham's English lecturer, but attended lectures widely and became a student of G. G. Coulton, among others. Although there is no record why she elected to apply to Newnham, a series of coincidences points to her fellowship. The Association of Collegiate Alumnae, founded in the United States in 1882, had an informal connection with the British Federation of University Women (BFUW), founded in 1907, of which Mrs. Henry Sidgwick, then principal of Newnham, was presi-dent. Further, Dr. Anna Paues, who was Swedish, is credited in the BFUW's fiftieth-anniversary history with having "enlisted the interest of Scandinavian countries" in the association, and she shared with Hope an interest in the *Ancrene Riwle*, on which she published a note in 1902. In time Carey Thomas also became active in the association, which in 1927 established a London headquarters at Crosby Hall, a fifteenth-century building not far from where Hope lived, where she sometimes took meals. Hope's acceptance at Newnham seems to have been one of the early successes of the connection between two associations, one American and one British, both dedicated to the cause of women's education, and both fighting an uphill battle in a not particularly sympathetic environment.

Apart from the general studies Hope undertook at Cambridge, she was committed to examining all of the manuscripts containing Richard Rolle's works with a view to establishing his canon. The term would become a year, a second year, and then a third. But in the summer of 1910 all that lay before her, and, with an additional sum from an aunt, she set out for a tour of England and its libraries with her mother.

The memory of Hope's first tour remained with her for the rest of her life, and the work she undertook during that trip was the beginning of her single greatest publication. She later dated the beginning of her scholarship from this time and, putting aside any thought of her projected Ph.D., insisted that it was then that her life as an independent scholar commenced. Years later, on June 30, 1952, she wrote to Ian Doyle of the "tour of England which my aunt gave me in the summer of 1910 before I settled in at manuscripts (Cambridge, London, Oxford), I had great pleasure in visiting Durham Cathedral and seeing the manuscripts. I think it may have been then that I had the great luck to be allowed to consult Canon [William] Greenwell [1820–1918] on the Rolle manuscript – he was then 90."

At the end of her tour she settled in Cambridge, though she was officially still attached to Radcliffe. The year 1910 was an extraordinary year in British constitutional history, with general elections in January and again in December, and Liberal reform, particularly the destruction of the power of the House of Lords and the limitation of the term of Parliament from seven years to five, hanging in the balance. On May 6, King Edward VII died, and the new king, the reliable, unbending George V, succeeded him, lending a sense of continuity to a period when major political disruptions were taking place. But Hope's political interests were decades in the future.

Her time at Newnham was important to her, and she made friends and contacts that she kept for the rest of her life. But in a more intimate way, too, she also came to know something of England, and something of her first reaction appears in her letter to the *Times* of 1928. Her first friends appear to have been Margaret Deanesly and Marietta Pallis. In Margaret (Peggy) Deanesly, a year her junior, Hope found her first close friend and collaborator, whom she advised and who also helped her. After taking a first-class degree in the Cambridge History Tripos, Margaret proceeded to take an M.A. at Manchester, before returning to Newnham. She also tried a brief period as a novice in Syon Abbey. Her subsequent career as a medieval historian was as distinguished as Hope's, and she was based in London, first at Royal Holloway, then at Bedford College, where she became professor in 1942. In 1950, many years and many books later, she retired. She died in 1977.

In 1912 she returned from Ireland, where, among other things, she had examined certain Richard Rolle manuscripts for Hope in Trinity College, Dublin, a service she also carried out in Oxford. Partly in return Hope sent her, along with a small hourly fee, a bibliography of Richard Rolle, which precipitated Margaret Deanesly's first scholarly project. For Hope the friendship, close when both were at Newnham, more distant later, was an important introduction to things English. Their correspondence, though markedly academic, also carries tidbits of gossip, like this, from Peggy to Hope in 1912: "Marietta is back from the Danube. I had a chaotic letter from her, and she has been buying crimson silk stockings in Paris."

Marietta Pallis was the closest friend Hope made during her years at Newnham, and one she kept. A lively, energetic student of botany, she, like Hope, was slightly older than most of their academic contemporaries, at a time of life when a year or two seems to matter. She came from an Anglo-Greek family in Liverpool, where her father, Alexander, who had previously worked in India and in Greece, was director of an important export-import firm dealing mainly with cotton, for which Liverpool's port was an important entry point. From him Marietta inherited a felt loyalty to Greece; in later years she would celebrate Greek independence day with enthusiasm, but her botanical studies had drawn her to the study of reeds, and it was to study them she had gone to the Danube. She cultivated other activities as well, in poetry and in painting, and it was through these interests that she established a close friendship with Hope. On November 25, 1911, Hope wrote to her parents from Cambridge, thanking them for money they had recently sent, and asking if there were any childhood photographs she could have: "Marietta wanted to see what I looked like as a little girl. She thinks them all hideous, very prim and plain (which is what I always told her I was)." The two would remain in contact throughout the war years, and during the 1920s and 1930s Hope lived with Marietta, at what became her permanent address in England, 116 Cheyne Walk, London SW 10.

Temperamentally the two young women were very unalike. A shared unconventionality did not hide the difference between the striking (but middle-sized) Marietta Pallis, direct, assertive, and self-willed; and Hope, slight (not much over five feet), studiously plain, quiet though expansive among friends, deferential but forceful, dedicated to her work. Hope's seriousness of mind she would have shared with her friend, and because

Marietta remained somewhat un-English in manner, the two slightly older and evidently "foreign" women would have had certain obvious bonds.

Other bonds were less obvious. One was creative writing, which both pursued at a time when they were also engaged in larger preoccupations, Hope's in medieval studies, Marietta's in botany; another was Norfolk. In certain of her poems, written for the most part in 1916–17, Marietta treated both her engagement with the countryside and also her many friendships, including her friendship with Hope. Her poems, which not infrequently echo Robert Bridges, are now preserved in a manuscript in her hand among the Allen family papers in Oneida. Their quality is somewhat uneven, though at their best they are effective and articulate. One of the best is "King's Water," written between July 17 and 20, 1916, which treats not only the Norfolk countryside but also the war during which it was written. I quote it here, together with the note with which Marietta Pallis introduced it, and a slightly later poem dedicated to Hope, who was by that time back in Oneida:

King's Water

The country people in Norfolk call the poppies soldiers. Carr is a wet wood of alder and birch; a pulk-hole is a water hole.

> There is a valley so flow'ry, so wet,
> Round it a circle of poppy-red hills,
> 'Soldiers,' 'Soldiers,' circle the vale,
> Gorgeous & brave in their scarlet.
>
> And in the valley there is a carr
> Not far from the scarlet soldiers
> Slant-growing birches, rotten & rank
> Root in the putrid black mire
>
> And in the carr there is a pulk,
> Dead, dead, a jewel entracing;
> And to it, lo! once came a king
> Parting the hop-hangings slowly.
>
> And the king's dead, heigho!
> Long, long ago,
> But the poppies glow,
> Blessed soldiers!

The other poem, dedicated to Hope, is called "May."

May

I smile at the grace of the cherry,
and the cherry smiled grace to me;
I blew a kiss to the cherry,
and the wind blew its petals to me:
with its delicate flakes I was whitened,
I loved, and the month was May.

And all through the burning summer,
and all through the winter's frost,
I see the white of the cherry,
The grace of the month of May;
and I live in the love of the cherry
that I'll kiss—and the month shall be May.

The poem reveals a degree of convention present in many of Marietta's other poems, and seems to indicate a longed-for, rather than a practised, intimacy. But it shows too a depth of feeling to which Hope, in the early days of their friendship, no doubt responded.

In many ways Marietta was a support to Hope. In May, 1912, Hope wished to examine a Richard Rolle manuscript at a theological library known as Dr. Williams's Library, in London, for which character references were required, and Marietta was one of the two persons to testify for her. The other was G. G. Coulton, the single most important intellectual influence she encountered in Cambridge.

In a description of her early work, now at Oxford, Hope reports "some kind assistance" she received from Dr. Paues, the English lecturer at Newnham, and adds that she "attended lectures . . . on medieval thought by Mr. Coulton." She also mentions having heard lectures by Arthur Woollgar Verrall and Sir William Ridgeway on Greek literature and archaeology. Yet among all of the influences she encountered at Cambridge, Coulton's was the greatest. In later years her association with a number of Benedictine, Franciscan, and Jesuit priests obscured the closeness of her early friendship with Coulton, with whom she always remained on friendly, though not intimate, terms. But Coulton was kind to her in her first days in Cambridge and in a difficult period that lay ahead. Hope's relationship with Coulton's wife was also close thoughout her life, no doubt influencing him too.

Hope's sensitivity to Coulton's view of the Middle Ages as violent, brutal, full of ecclesiastical corruption and misdeed yet capable of sublime beauty, may have restrained her from articulating her own more cogent and sympathetic view of the period, but Coulton's attention to detail, to primary sources, and his insistence on accurately quoted texts influenced her most mature work. To compare Hope's article on the *Prick of Conscience* of 1910 with her articles on the *Ancrene Riwle* of 1917 and 1918 is to witness a change in intensity that is also a change in substance, an intellectual coming of age. Her initial interest, certain major texts, her enthusiasm for some ideas, for literature, and for manuscripts may have been inspired by Carleton Brown and Bryn Mawr, but her methodology hardened when she came under Coulton's determined, even grinding, influence in Cambridge.

Thus it was under Coulton that she came to commit herself to reasoned and argued judgments, not simply to the discovery and reporting of fact and inference. No doubt she would have come to this in time, but exposure to the sort of reasoning Coulton demanded was an advantage to one schooled thus far to admire, not analyze. An example of Coulton's influence can be seen in Hope's treatment of the (not uncommon) name William of Nassington in her *Prick of Conscience* article of 1910. Hope noted six times that the name appeared in contemporary documents of the period and was rightly cautious of assuming that all six referred to the Yorkshire ecclesiastical *advocatus* who in about 1375 may have translated the *Speculum vitae* into English. In this instance her caution may have been too pronounced. She seemed willing to concede that Master William de Nassington, the king's clerk who was given a benefice in Chichester in 1344–45, was a different man from the William of Nassington who resigned in 1352 from his Chichester benefice. A decade late this identification would not have troubled Hope for an instant; there are times when, reading her later work on the *Ancrene Riwle*, one wishes for a little of her earlier caution, but the ability to come to a conclusion and to make it stick she learned from Coulton. But Coulton might not have understood the real reason she rejected Rolle's authorship of the *Prick of Conscience*: in her view the author "had no concept of mystical theory." But he saw that

Hope's cautious and sensitive mind should be made critical. Although some of Coulton's own work would have benefited from Hope's fine discrimination, it is impossible not to conclude, as she did, that she learned much from his teaching. The fierceness of his comments on other scholars suggests one reason for the distance the two observed both at the time and in later life. One never treats a really formidable mind with nonchalance.

A second association that Hope developed during her early years at Cambridge was with Sir William A. Craigie (he became a Knight Commander in 1930); it became one of the longest-lasting associations of her career. Craigie, seventeen years her senior, was a Scottish philologist and lexicographer of great distinction, one of the early editors of The New (later Oxford) English Dictionary. Formerly professor of Latin in Saint Andrews University, since 1915 he had been Rawlinson and Bosworth Professor of Anglo-Saxon at Oxford. He was known not only for his evident learning (his work on Scottish, Frisian, Gaelic and especially Icelandic is still used) but also for the courtesy of his address and his ability, rare in its time, to deal with women as serious scholars and as colleagues. The "List of Subscribers" in his memoire and bibliography of 1952 contains the names of more women than most of his contemporaries could have mustered, and his correspondence with Hope, preserved at Bryn Mawr, shows not only his learning but also the formal generosity with which he imparted it. He spent the last ten years of his working life at the University of Chicago, from which he retired in 1936. He was for Hope a sane balance to Coulton's ideological intransigence.

Craigie's direct influence on Hope was most evident in two areas, in her work on the Dictionary of Modern English at the Universtiy of Michigan in the 1930s, and in her folklore publications, which for the most part concentrated on the cultural connotations and denotations of certain words. This aspect of Craigie's work emerges, for example, in a tract (no. 27) he wrote at Chicago in 1927 for the Society for Pure English, a philological group somewhat more innovative and interesting than its badly chosen name suggests, organized by Robert Bridges and others in 1913 and restarted after the war. The tract was entitled The Study of American English, a topic that would have caught Hope's eye. It shows a breadth of cultural interest and a willingness to admit linguistic change together with a desire to fix meaning as closely as possible, typical of the society's best tracts. It concludes with a glossary containing certain words (like *Bogus* and *Bed bug*) that seem to anticipate certain of Hope's later interests, and shows a concern for current usage and for literary allusion that she would likewise develop.

A third intellectual interest during this period may have been less important in fixing her methods but clearly informed her attitudes toward the Middle Ages, and toward England. While she was at Cambridge, she came to know Mirfield Father Canon Walter H. Frere, a distinguished Church of England scholar of medieval liturgy and later bishop of Truro, in Cornwall, who from 1911 directed by correspondence (now in the Bryn Mawr collection) her study of liturgy at a formative period of her development. A letter of Frere's dated June 15, 1911 answers a question of Hope's on the Holy Name, a devotion Rolle precipitated, and perhaps began, in England, that continued to interest Hope throughout her working life. He pointed to a reference, misleadingly reported in a modern edition of the Sarum Breviary, and referred her to the question of the Holy Name in the primers and in the service books of York and of Sarum. Then as now the history of the Psalter remained to be written, but the books were, as Frere remarked, of real importance for understanding the facts of medieval devotion. He pointed to a list of Oxford primers in a publication of his own and offered her a list of Cambridge primers, if that would be of use. The view of the Middle Ages implied in this objective, reasoned and humane letter was perhaps somewhat at odds with the view she would have gleaned from Coulton, but in the end it was more influential.

One searches Hope's correspondence in vain throughout this period for any interest in the larger social issues of the moment. Her concern for Ireland, then and later, seems not to have embraced home rule but to have been limited to the Trinity College manuscript of the Dublin Rule. Her familial associations with the management and operation of the Oneida factories would not have disposed her to view sympathetically the emergence of the Parliamentary Labour party, decisive as that event was for the future of modern Britain. But one other event of signal importance would not have escaped her notice, and that was the new direction which the woman suffrage movement had recently taken. In 1910, the year of Hope's first trip to Britain, the movement, ably led by Mrs. Emmeline Pankhurst and her daughters Christabel and Sylvia, turned to what can only seem now a very moderate violence to gain their great goal, votes for women.

The date of the beginning of the new offensive was November 18, 1910, "Black Friday," when members of Mrs. Pankhurst's Women's Social and Political Union (WSPU) came into conflict with the police in Parliament Square. But the battle that ensued was nothing compared to events of the next year, when, on November 21, a group of women smashed windows in the Home Office, the War Office, the Foreign Office, the Board of Education, the Treasury, Somerset House, and other buildings. The division between the militant and the non-militant suffragettes became even clearer the next summer when, under orders from Christabel Pankhurst, now settled beyond the law's reach in Paris, arson, directed mostly against unoccupied country houses and remote parish churches, became the tactics and the topics of the hour.

The campaign continued with increasing fervor and destruction until 1914, when Lord Herbert Asquith's government, urged on, it must be said, by the attention the emerging Labour party was paying to the movement, conceded its support to Sylvia Pankhurst's East London Federation, a group recently expelled from the WSPU for setting aside the class bias under which most of the suffragettes operated and forming an alliance with the working class, and with men. Votes for women would not come until 1918, and then only for women over thirty. The fear was less immaturity than numbers: women outnumbered men, and Parliament was evidently concerned about being turned out en masse. Full suffrage came in 1928 and no doubt contributed to the Labour victory the next year.

During the early militant period of the suffragette movement Hope Allen, a student of medieval history and literature at Newnham College, Cambridge, was separated by nationality and by sensibility from the activities of the WSPU. No student of Carey Thomas and of Bryn Mawr would have failed to remark its existence and its mode of operation, but Hope had a temperamental aversion to what she took to be extremity of whatever sort, an aversion that may have owed something to her Oneida background. Though certain in her own mind that women's causes were both necessary and right, she would have been disinclined to join, or perhaps even to sympathize with, the WSPU. Even so, it is clear that the suffrage movement itself brought home to her the difficulties women experienced in England, where she herself was enjoying relatively greater freedom. Put another way, its existence made her present undertakings a matter of principle: it was right to be a woman and a scholar, right to set aside confrontation in favor of learning, but not right to abandon the study of women's past.

In this period too, Hope's study of Richard Rolle was deepening, while her interest in the *Ancrene Riwle* and in the whole range of problems associated with women recluses remained. These were not, to be sure, concerns with which the Pankhursts would have much sympathized, but in a way they were Hope's answer to the challenge posed by the WSPU. She was not indifferent to the role of women, but neither was she immediately attracted to the simple and somewhat class-bound consciousness on which the movement rested. As first Sylvia and then Christabel Pankhurst came to appreciate, votes for women was only part of a larger issue. And it was this larger issue, in its historical as well as its present aspect, that engaged Hope's attention. Scholarship and England were rapidly becoming one for her, and if the issues of the moment did not engage her interest, less immediate ones did. Her concern was for women's issues, for the powers of the only apparently weak, in particular for mystics, anchoresses, saints. Though they were not reformers in the narrow sense, they nevertheless altered profoundly the perceptions and attitudes into which they were born.

Later in life Hope took an acute interest in the politics of the day, moderating her Republican conservatism to embrace Franklin D. Roosevelt and even Walter Lippmann. But her Cambridge years were occupied with other matters. During that time her intellectual powers developed along with her academic interests. In the end they drew her to a settled, even a profound, interest in the role of women in medieval English society and in the alternative system of values that their religion held out, alternative to the more repressive social patterns of their day, and also of later times. In these matters Hope sacrificed nothing of her scholarship to feminist interest, and she was always strictly impartial in her judgments. She believed passionately in the existence of objective, empirical answers to virtually every question, and that belief, among many, helped make her time in Cambridge important, as later accomplishments were to prove.

Urged on by academic considerations, and by the opportunities for close, demanding textual scholarship that British libraries offer a dedicated young student, Hope Allen plunged into her task: the examination of every manuscript containing a work thought to have been written by Richard Rolle. She began with manuscripts in Cambridge but rapidly moved on to manuscripts in London. There she settled into the Lonsdale Hotel, then in Montague Place, close to the British Museum, from which she wrote to her parents on February 1, 1911: "This house is within pleasant walking distance of hosts of interesting places. I can get to all the open-air bookshops, and be assured whether it's dark or not.—or to the river, or the Inns of Court, or 'the city' etc. I haven't begun to consult my Baedeker much yet."

It was probably during this time too that she met the man who would have the greatest immediate impact on her study of manuscripts, John Alexander Herbert, deputy keeper in the manuscript department of the British Museum, who became her fast friend. Born in 1862, Herbert entered the department in 1887 and by 1910 had published catalogues of the manuscripts of romances and of the Titus and Vespasian Cotton manuscripts in the museum. He was one of those English scholars who, largely self-taught, became remarkably learned and able and whose contemporary reputation, based on specialist knowledge of his abilities, went well beyond what could be gathered from his publications. His chief at the British Museum, Sir George Warner, who had assisted in his training, had utmost confidence in his abilities; and a wide range of scholars, from M. R. James, who trusted Herbert's advice in cataloguing the Yates Thompson manuscripts, to Kenneth Sisam, who came to know Herbert during the years he spent in London, agreed. Through Herbert Hope came to know, with differing degrees of closeness, many of the scholars who worked at the British Museum.

Herbert was the second husband of the essayist Alice Herbert, by whom he had one child; there were three stepchildren. One of the daughters of Mrs. Herbert's first marriage, Ivy Low, would marry, much to her parents' surprise, Maxim Litvinov, the Soviet ambassador to Britain before and briefly during World War II. Alice Herbert's novel *A Pen and Ink Passion* (1927) includes sketches of her husband and their circle; *Heaven and Charing Cross* (1922) reflects their conversion to Roman Catholicism. She died in 1941, seven years before her husband, and Hope wrote a moving obituary of this old but not particularly close friend. Her drafts of the obituary (now in Oxford) commend Ivy Lit-vinov's London entertainments and recall that she shopped at Fortnum's.

Herbert's taste was refined, but informed by the conventions of his day. His *Illuminated Manuscripts*, published for "the Conoisseur's Library" in 1911, is a learned and substantial work, which, however, rejects Anglo-Saxon illumination as showing "little sense of proportion or design" and remarks of the Bodleian Library's manuscript MS Junius 11 that "all attempts to represent the nude are of course disastrous.... Adam and Eve only become endurable when the Fall has driven them to adopt the wrinkled draperies which leave room for the cunning convolutions of the Anglo-Saxon line." Herbert believed that "the first quarter of the four-teenth century was the real flowering-time of English Illumination," for it was only then that "a peculiarly satisfying balance" which combined "realism, imagination and tradition, illumination and ornament" was formed. This kind of appreciation owed much to John Ruskin, and its strictures on Anglo-Saxon illumination now seem particularly dated; but against the popular assumption of Renaissance superiority, it is worth noticing the esteem in which the early fourteenth century was held by art historians and other medieval scholars about the time Hope began work-ing in the period. To many academics in the early twentieth century, the period of Richard Rolle was the first great flowering of English culture.

Hope and Herbert's work together (collaboration is not too strong a word) began in earnest in 1921, when Hope settled in London, but their first meeting dates from the earlier period when Hope was beginning to explore, for the first time, the riches of the libraries about her. Her pleasure in her discoveries, together with the respect and courtesy accorded women scholars in Britain, persuaded her to delay her return to America for at least a year. She wrote to Dean Coes at Radcliffe reporting her decision, since the task of examining Rolle manuscripts, done prop-erly, had hardly begun, and, after due consideration, rejected the offer of a readership in English at Bryn Mawr, ("$800 the first year, $900 the second and $1000 the third") which came to her from Carey Thomas in a letter dated June 12, 1911. Her decision not to return to her alma mater was an important one and set the seal on what would become her career, that of an independent scholar, though she can hardly have known that at the time. That the offer was repeated about two years later, when, as it proved, there was even less chance of acceptance, suggests that Hope pleaded that the present state of her work would not allow her to return. But it is possible too that the attractions of scholarship, as well as the pleasures of life in England, had already made clear to her where her true vocation lay.

During this period she published a few short studies that showed the direction of her research and her thinking. In the German journal *Archiv* (volume 127 for 1911), she noted the influence of the *Speculum vitae* on the Middle English poem "The Desert of Religion," which the journal had recently published. In the *Modern Language Review* for January, 1912, she noted an echo of Pseudo-Dionysius in Tennyson's lines "For so the whole wide earth is bound / With golden chains about the feet of God." Neither article was a major contribution, but each showed an active and engaged mind already at work, already aware of the distinction between what was known and what was not. The Tennyson note, the only study on that poet in her career, shows too an awareness of what had larger relevance in her medieval work and would please editors.

One other article she wrote about this time appeared in the *Athenaeum* for August 23, 1913, by which time she was back in America. At Emmanuel College, Cambridge, Manuscript 35 contains the marginal notes of one John Norton, whom Hope, following Laura Hibbard, identified as the treasurer of York Cathedral (d. 1414). The notes appear in a manuscript of Rolle's *Incendium amoris* and appear to imply that Norton copied his manuscript from one written in Rolle's own hand. The identification of Norton has since been disputed, but what particularly took Hope's attention was the name and monograph of Joanna Sewell, a nun of the Bridgittine convent of Syon Abbey, on a manuscript that also bears the monogram of James Greenhalgh, the cleric with whom, as we shall see, Joanna was intimately associated. In fact, the manuscript may not have been as closely associated with Rolle as Norton, writing in the fifteenth century, believed. Carthusian origin would equally account for its transmission, but with a generosity rare in a young scholar Hope relinquished the publication of the text to her Newnham friend Margaret Deanesly, whose edition, with an acknowledgment to Hope, appeared from the University of Manchester in 1915. Deanesly further acknowledged the assistance of Rotha Mary Clay, whom Hope came soon to know, and the lady abbess of Syon Abbey, whom Hope met in her company.

In early February, 1912, Hope experienced a breakdown which seems to have been largely physical, due in part to overwork. Her letters to her family reporting on her convalescence are lively. "I am leaving the future open," she wrote on February 13, "and not bothering about it, knowing I am very well situated for the present. If however when I get up it seems best for me to go home to finish my rest, it will make all the difference in my mind to be assured that I can return to finish. I don't think Dr. Rogers will let me do anything rash."

She moved from Cambridge to stay with friends in Barton, not far away, from which she wrote again on the twentieth:

> The doctor came out today to see me for the first time. He thought me distinctly better, but that I must continue on the same way for a time longer. The massage will continue to strengthen my digestion and my muscles. He thought me fatter and I am sure I am – I really feel much better and am distinctly encouraged. Honestly I realize that I had better lie a little while longer because I can't do much yet, and I still dream a good deal, and have more or less discomfort now and then in my digestion and flatuency. It is certainly curious that I have been "let in" for this long rest.

She remained in the country for two months, constantly reporting progress home during the period. To Radcliffe she wrote with greater attention to the effect of the illness on her work, remarking in a March 3 letter to Dean Coes, that the doctor "has continued to keep me on childish stipends of work – in very short measure – only now within the last fortnight have I reached the allowance of three and a half hours a day." By this time she had plans to return to America and to accompany her mother to Phoenix, Arizona, for a rest. By May she was in London, en route home.

The causes of Hope's breakdown were undoubtedly complex and related to earlier illnesses. To Radcliffe she remarked, in postponing her doctor's degree "I haven't been well and still am resting. Various accidents which befell in the summer when I was travelling knocked me up more or less and I haven't been quite well since." When Dean Coes wrote to her adviser, Professor Schofield (Hope had written to Kittredge her-

37

self), he wrote regretting the breakdown and urging her to abandon work on Rolle in favor of a less complicated project on the *Ancrene Riwle.*

When Hope returned to America in the summer of 1912, she clearly expected to return to England in relatively short order and to complete her thesis on Rolle. In fact she did neither. She accompanied her mother to Arizona for a rest, but it was she, not her mother, who most benefited. When they returned home her mother was clearly in failing health and could not be left again. On September 20, 1913, she died. Hope's own health had improved from the previous winter, but was, as always, precarious. She took charge of her father's household and attended to such details as she could. During this time her academic work stopped. No doubt the research on Rolle had to since she was too far from the libraries she needed, and not strong enough in any case. But she also stopped writing the kinds of short studies she took pleasure in during her scholarly career, and it seems possible that the period was a difficult one for her.

By 1914 she had taken up her scholarly activities again; in September of that year she wrote to Rotha Mary Clay, the author of a recent (and still useful) work on medieval hermits, asking about a reference that she believed to be relevant to her work on Rolle. It was two years before she had an answer; her letter was apparently mislaid, but it was answered soon after Hope again appeared in print, which suggests that Rotha Clay, busy with war work, may have needed a reminder. But it was primarily the war which prevented her return to scholarly work: in August, 1914, England declared war on Germany, and civilian travel was curtailed. Thereafter a mixture of prudence, familial injunction, and ill health kept Hope at home.

But she was not inactive. In 1912 she had commenced her recovery in Oneida by taking a closer look at the land around her, and during this period she came to know well several members of the Oneida Indian tribe. Years later, in some notes (now preserved in Syracuse) on tribe members, she recalled that it was during this period that her friendships with them grew. More than twenty years later she published some of the mythological tales that her Oneida friends, Anna and Si Johnson, told her during this period (we shall return to them in chapter 6), and that she began to record in 1917. She claimed a special bond with the Johnsons, who had brought her family a baby cariage for her shortly after her birth, but their rediscovery she carefully dated to 1912, when she returned to Oneida to complete recovery from her breakdown.

During this period too she began to write again. Initially she wrote nonfiction, producing the first version of "Relics," her unpublished account of Oneida community culture, which she rewrote off and on for the next twenty years. But soon she turned to more scholarly work. She took up certain Anglo-Norman texts that had attracted her years before, and turned again to the *Ancrene Riwle*. In 1917 she published in *Modern Philology* "A Note on the *Lamentation of Mary*," in which she identified the Anglo-Norman and Latin sources of that work, and "A Note on the *Proverbs of Prophets, Poets and Saints*," in which she pointed out yet more Anglo-Norman sources. Both are signed from Kenwood, New York (her earlier publications had been signed from Cambridge), and she appears to have hesitated to fix Oneida, with its still somewhat ambiguous cultural connotations, as her permanent address, a hesitation, if indeed it existed, that she soon thrust aside. Both notes show a scholar's pleasure in discovery. It is important to know the sources of Middle English works in order to understand the degree of their originality, and this the notes accomplish. They also show how her work was now focusing on Anglo-Norman literature, no doubt in part a result of the course in Old French she had taken at Radcliffe.

Her first long article to see print was "*The Manuel des Pechiez* and the Scholastic Prologue," which appeared in the *Romanic Review* for 1917. In the article she treated what she took to be a prologue in that Anglo-Norman work, and her suggestion, based, it must be said, on a misreading, stood for twenty-two years before being corrected by E. J. F. Arnould in the *Modern Language Review* for 1939, which pointed out that line 351 of that work, which was the basis for Hope's argument, did not refer to a prologue of the *Manuel*, but meant simply, "The Prologue shall be found further on in the book." But Arnould carefully praised Hope's "many judicious and original remarks on various issues connected with the *Manuel*." In subsequent articles she brought her knowledge of Anglo-Norman to bear on Middle English literature.

In 1918 she published two important articles, one in volume 9 of *Romanic Reiew* on what she called the mystical lyrics of the *Manuel des Pechiez*, the other in volume 33 of *PMLA* on the thirteenth-century work the *Ancrene Riwle*. The first article concerned two Anglo-Norman lyrics found at the end of the thirteenth-century *Manuel des Pechiez*, whch did not appear in the familiar Middle English version of Robert Mannyng of Brunne in the next century, but which she identified as having influenced other Middle English lyrics. The real purpose of her article, however, was "to show that a movement towards mysticism was especially evident in England before the great mystical outburst of the later Middle Ages, general throughout Europe" (p. 193). She sought primarily to establish this "outburst" in Latin, English, and Anglo-Norman texts, claiming for the last a closeness to Middle English, together with certain peculiarly English characteristics, and thus insisting on a greater degree of English influence in the development of medieval mysticism than most scholars of the time recognized. Her analysis placed a great weight on two slender lyrics, but she was convinced that the main sources of English inspiration were French and that a quality she called "mysticism" could be discovered in their influence.

She wrote:

> When in the thirteenth-century, which was not especially mystical in France, we find French lyrics written in England already showing strong currents of mysticism that was to produce the creative English mystics of the fourteenth century, it cannot be said that this branch of Anglo-Norman literature was mainly imitative of French models. The fourteenth-century in France has been described as especially unmystical, and it is a similar trick of fortune that has brought into the history of French medieval literature a considerable body of mystical verse, written in French by Englishmen, because England has not yet thrown off the habit, acquired at the Conquest, of using French. These writers, in spite of their medium, were expressing the native influences that led their countrymen in the next century to follow the examples of their Teutonic relatives in an outburst of creative mysticism (pp. 165–66).

The lyrics in the *Manuel* then "to some degree prophesy the immediate future of English religious devotion," giving to the student "a hint that the beginning of the English mystical movement of the fourteenth century must be sought in part, at least, amidst the Anglo-Norman literature of the thirteenth."

The remarks are of significance for her later work, as are some of the corollaries she established: what she called the English emphasis on devotion to Christ, particularly in his Passion (rather than to Mary), and the importance she early attached to the devotion of the Holy Name. This devotion she later associated in its popularity, though not in its origin, with Richard Rolle. This early concern for the "Englishness" of British medieval spirituality never left her, and when she turned to consider other influences, she felt constrained to point out that "no racial divisions" (by which she meant between Norman and English) existed in England as late as the time of composition of the *Manuel des Pechiez*" (pp. 170–71), and was particularly critical of the *Cambridge History of English Literature* (I:384) for suggesting that the *Manuel* was "written, probably, for Norman settlers in Yorkshire."

Turning to the broader influences of Anglo-Norman culture on the English, she pointed to writers who would be of considerable importance for her later work, Anselm, and, following him, a group of spiritual texts associated with Richard Rolle, of which *A Talking of the Love of God* seemed to her the most significant: "The whole development of English mysticism may be indicated in (its) genealogy," she suggested, remarking too that "the style of this production, no less than the substance, seems to fall in direct line from Anselm" (p. 187). Between Anselm and the fourteenth century Hope noted "two general religious revivals," the coming of the Cistercians and the coming of the Friars. The Cistercian influence she found important for the development of mysticism, particularly in the person of Ælred of Riveaux, whose influence she believed to have been great. But she was concerned too with the founding of the native Gilbertine order, "the only English order founded at any period," (p. 189), which was associated with the tradition of mystical awareness, a tradition that led to the *Ancrene Riwle*. The Gilbertine order, was founded by Saint Gilbert of Sempringham (ca. 1083–1189), a parish priest who had encouraged seven laywomen of his congregation to adopt a distinctive rule of life, which Gilbert himself may have sanctioned; his own order was indeed the only British order eventually sanctioned by Rome in the medieval period. Hope followed a source that reported that Gilbert always carried with him the key to the building in which the women were enclosed; she also believed (wrongly) that Gilbert was a lay landowner. Whatever the precise circumstances of its founding, in time the group of lay sisters joined in time with a group of lay brothers, who assisted with the manual work of the community. In 1148 the Cistercians at Citeaux declined to incorporate the community of women into its rule, and thereafter it was governed, through Gilbert's direction, by the Canons Regular, who followed the rule of Saint Augustine. The order rapidly developed a double structure of houses, one for Canons only, the other for both men and women. By the time of Gilbert's death in 1189 it maintained nine double houses, four for Canons only; at the time of the dissolution of monasteries there were twenty-five houses in all.

It may be that Hope Allen intended to identify the Gilbertine order with the origin of the *Ancrene Riwle*, but in her 1918 *PMLA* article she subsequently set the Gilbertine associations aside, and when she came to propose Kilburn as the source for the *Ancrene Riwle*, she noted only that "the Gilbertine order took its rise at about the time of the establishment of Kilburn in a 'church anchorage' of much the same type as that described in the *Riwle* and in the records at Kilburn" (p. 479, n. 8). Not all of her information about Gilbert was accurate, but the importance of the Augustine Canons in the creation of the *Ancrene Riwle* was an important attribution, and one that has lasted.

These Canons were a loose-knit group of clerics dedicated to a common life of poverty, chastity, and obedience, following the primitive practice of the Church as they understood it. Approved by the Lateran synods of 1059 and 1063, they were known by the early twelfth century as Canons Regular ("Regular" because they followed a rule, in their case that of Saint Augustine, which had become widely known in the eleventh century). Subsequently they were influenced by Cistercian customs, and, as a clerical order, were subject to ecclesiastical visitation. But they retained a degree of flexibility in the organization of individual houses and undertook a range of responsibilities, both active and contemplative.

Hope's interest in little-studied aspects of devout spirituality, which was to become one of her most important contributions to medieval studies, found its fullest expression thus far in her 1918 *PMLA* article cited above. In the same volume Charlotte D'Evelyn, an instructor in English at Mount Holyoke College, in Massachusetts, and a lifelong friend of Hope's, published "The Middle-English Metrical Version of the *Revelations of Methodius*; with a Study of the Influence of Methodius in Middle English Writings," (pp. 135–203), and together the two articles, each of substantial length, helped establish the importance of late-medieval devotional texts that had hitherto been little studied.

Hope's own contribution was the more important of the two. Entitled "The Origin of the *Ancrene Riwle*" it was the first study of real importance by an American scholar to appear on the subject. The *Riwle* is a prose text preserved in seventeen manuscripts (nine in English, four in French, and four in Latin), and the complex relationships among these versions is even now a subject of dispute. Of the quality of the work, however, there is no debate at all. "The Rule for Anchoresses" is one of the most attractive pieces of early Middle English literature, and among contemporary religious texts it has no equal. A work steeped in the spirituality of the twelfth century (though probably composed early in the thirteenth), *Ancrene Riwle* is divided into eight parts, treating "Devotion," "The Custody of the Senses," "The Custody of the Heart," "Temptation," "Confession," "Penance," "Love," and the rule the enclosed sisters were to follow.

Throughout the work the demands of the spiritual life are tempered with a sensitivity toward human frailty. Encouraging and supporting though it is, however, *Ancrene Riwle* is still a guide to the spiritual life written by a man for a woman; or, according to its attestation, for three women. Its tone is paternal and admonitory: the anchoresses are young saplings in God's orchard; they should try to avoid the sight of a human face and meditate on Christ, on Mary, above all, on the Passion. The author would rather see them hanged on a gibbet than kiss a man. Put in these terms the text sounds too daunting; in fact, it is a humane and reasoned document. Throughout, it takes the tone of conversation, the *sermo generalis*, maintaining a dignified and even courteous tenor of address. At its best its style is brilliant; there is nothing as good in English prose before, and not for a long while after. The balance, allusiveness, restraint, and conviction appear now and again in twelfth-century Latin texts, but in English, never.

Nor was its style its only attraction. Written by a man for a woman it may have been, but it showed a sensitivity toward gender rare in its time, and concerned itself with a whole range of devotional practices designed to assist, not to compel, spiritual development. The Maria psalms, the night prayers, the Hours of the Holy Ghost, all figured in the spiritual program. For a historian it is markedly valuable, for the student of spirituality it is hardly less so. The work examines the warm and urgent depth of feeling of those who elect the spiritual life. It explores the variety of responses that life calls up and the demands it makes. It concerns itself with the individual rather than with the group or the community, and focuses on *her* introspection, habits of mind, and attitudes of meditation, thought and behavior. It is not so much about techniques of control as about those of discovery, and the male voice that sounds throughout is finally less commanding than following, its speaker observing a course that the young women, true to their own desires, are charting by themselves.

These circumstances may suggest too that there are real difficulties involved in any identification of those to whom the "original" *Ancrene Riwle* was directed. Many of the sources, after all, are learned and yet seem to be tempered by the author's experience in the kind of spiritual direction with which the work is concerned. It is the product not of a spiritual director new to his work but of one who, in his confident handling of a range of learned and spiritual sources, knows what can be expected. It is also a work which has survived in a surprisingly large number of manuscripts, widely distributed. These facts together may suggest that the "three young women" to whom the work is apparently directed may have been something of a polite fiction and that the *Riwle* is in fact intended to serve as a spiritual handbook for any group of young women, and their director, cloistered if need be, but in need of direction in any case. Certain of the injunctions in it (as those against kissing and keeping cats) seem to reach out beyond an immediate group to the larger responsibilities of those who wish to engage the life of the spirit. The work as a whole has a paradigmatic character that seems an intrinsic part of the author's intention, an intention founded on the experiences of a group of young women, certainly, but probably not confined to one group. Quite apart from the improbability of a confessor (for so the author seems to have been) detailing the identity of his charges, the work contains echoes of a medieval genre common enough later on: the instructions of a spiritual director to his young charge, who in practice was both anony-mous and imaginary. The distribution of the manuscripts suggests not only early popularity but also a willingness to share what was evidently composed with an eye for dissemination to an informed and (from the range of authorities employed) critical audience: devout women no doubt, and also their directors.

Alternatively, some of the details may have been real, some invented.

The rule may have been conceived of for a specific community or at least a specific purpose, but written down with a larger audience in mind. If such were the circumstances, it is now very difficult to separate the actual from the fictitious, though the number of women involved is one of the more likely candidates for invention, however experienced in the ways of spiritual direction the author may have been. In her many years of working on the *Ancrene Riwle*, Hope found very few communities of women containing only three members, and though she herself never questioned the group's existence as described, it is possible, it seems to me, to entertain a doubt.

These suggestions (they are only that) do not lessen the contribution that Hope Allen made to the understanding of the text, though her approach was altogether different. Concerned for the spirituality of the work, she achieved a real breakthrough by first asking not "Who wrote the *Ancrene Riwle*?" (though she would come to that in time) but "For whom was it written?" She saw at once that it was concerned with the spiritual state of an intelligent, perceptive, and feeling group of young women, and that it was to them that attention should be directed. Still, she stood at a great disadvantage: she had only James Morton's Camden Society edition of 1853, which printed the text preserved in British Library Cotton Manuscript Nero A xiv, and some rotographs of a French translation. These were complicated by the fact that in 1918 neither the date nor the original language of the work was understood. Following a recent article, Hope reluctantly accepted that the original language had probably been French, from which the English was a translation, but we now know that the reverse is in fact the case. Similarly, the date of the work was uncertain in 1918, and it is not established even now. Hope proposed an early-twelfth-century date and further identified the young women in question as three nobly born sisters, Christina, Emma, and Gunhilda, who had lived enclosed in the early 1130s at the Priory of Kilburn, near London, a dependency of Westminster Abbey, to which the sisters were attached under one Godwyn, "magister loci."

Kilburn Priory, a subject to which Hope returned repeatedly throughout her working life, was a twelfth-century religious foundation established in the parish of Hampstead, Middlesex, on a site now covered, in all probability, by Saint Mary's Church, Priory Road. During the construction of Saint Mary's in the early 1850s, a number of medieval tiles and some human bones were unearthed. But the only illustration of the earlier priory is an eighteenth-century engraving from a lost drawing of 1722, that shows an unusually large structure attached to the priory church at the east end. But the building itself would probably have dated from the late, relatively affluent, days of Kilburn, after it had acquired social standing and local significance. Of the earlier foundation that so interested Hope Allen, no physical evidence remains. But it was to this Augustinian house attached to the Benedictine community of Westminster, that Hope directed her attention, and its first inhabitants, Christine, Emma, and Gunhilda, she came to identify with those for whom the *Ancrene Riwle* was written. More important than these identifications, which have not stood the test of time, was her larger analysis of the work itself, and her insistence, by inference, that such an analysis was important to the future of English studies.

Her suggestions, however, were sometimes mistaken, and so some of them appeared to certain of her contemporaries. In her early days as a scholar, for example, she sometimes assumed that everything which might have been probably had been. Thus, when discussing, in her 1918 *PMLA* article, the visit that Peter the Venerable made to Britain in 1130, she emphasized Peter's interest in the Convent of Mareigny (which included anchoresses), remarking that the conversations Peter had "may have" included "plans for Kilburn" (p. 528). Yet if her narrower ascriptions are sometimes open to doubt, her larger assumptions and suggestions are often perceptive and convincing. The point behind the improbable linking of Peter and Kilburn was to stress the degree to which Peter's spirituality finds expression in the *Ancrene Riwle*. Hope was seeking not only to indicate a source but also to document what she came to call the work's "environment":

> At the middle of the twelfth century—in religion, philosophy, and the arts, one of the most creative periods in history—the liberal party of the church evidently combined an unusual elasticity as to the forms of religious life with a most intense concern to avoid hypocrisy. . . . Consequently the forms of monasticism that gained its special affection were those, like the life of a Carthusian or of an anchorite, in which, according to the phrase of the time, the members lived "in a sepulchre." This somewhat unusual combination of ideas appears in the *Riwle*. To understand the full contemporary meaning of the work, we must read the letters of Peter the

Venerable; and we must read the *Ancrene Riwle* to understand the spirit that actuated Abbot Herbert to bestow the goods of his abbey to per-petuity, on persons of the other sex who did not even come under the title of his order. The sectarianism common to all ages was for a moment in abeyance, for the inspirational importance attached to differences in usage in that age of the rise of many orders had stimulated the liberals of that generation to special magnaminity (p. 533).

The reference to magnanimity follows from Hope's characterization of Kilburn as a Benedictine house following an Augustinian rule, a circum-stance she explained in the *Modern Language Review* in 1921. She conjectured that the abbot of Westminster had allowed the first master of Kilburn, perhaps a secular priest, to determine the choice of rule his order was to follow because he "had formulated that usage in a treatise which his abbey was proud to honor," as she later expressed it. Quite apart from the improbably early date, the problem with the choice of rules points to another weakness of the Kilburn theory, but it shows too the clarity and frankness with which Hope Allen addressed her text. She saw at once what the best critics have acknowledged: the degree of humanness that characterizes the document. The origin of this quality she found in monastic contention, particularly in the struggle between the Cistercians (whom she called, following G. G. Coulton, the "Puritans of the Middle Ages") and Peter the Venerable, who defended the older Benedictine tradition and did so in the context of admiration for the Carthusian ideal, which also, in Hope Allen's judgment, influenced the *Ancrene Riwle*. The mixed spirituality in the *Riwle* included both strict demands on conduct (and a consequent freedom from hypocrisy) and a humane adaptation to the needs of the young women concerned.

It is possible to believe, no doubt, that there are echoes of Bryn Mawr in this analysis and that the interest Hope Allen took in the *Ancrene Riwle* sprang from echoes she recognized in her own intellectual background. It was against this circumstance that her analysis would provide a learned and spirited defense of the importance and the probity of the work itself. It argued, if implicitly, for the centrality of the tradition that the *Ancrene Riwle* represented and pointed to a confluence of important European influences on every page. This learned and perceptive reading is still with us and still influences every important reading of the text. Yet it would not have threatened those contemporary scholars, G. G. Coulton for example, who remained convinced of the corruption of the late medieval church: here was an institution that had set its face against the hypocrisy, so the argument might run, which flourished everywhere. The argument proceeded with evident learning and objectivity, and most of her contemporaries learned much from her references and allusions, a fact which served to support her argument further.

The year 1924 was important for *Ancrene Riwle* studies for two reasons. In that year *Essays and Studies*, the journal of the English Association, published an important study by Miss D. M. E. Dymes which all but proved that the original language of the text was not French, as had earlier been thought, but almost certainly English. Also during 1924 Professor R. W. Chambers, of the University of London, completed an important study which he called "Recent Research upon the *Ancrene Riwle*," and published in the first issue of the new *Review of English Studies*, which appeared in January, 1925. That a scholar of Chambers' standing would publish an article on the topic was an attestation of the importance that the work had assumed, an importance for which Hope Allen's work was in large measure responsible. After treating Macauley and Dymes, it was to "Miss Allen" that Chambers turned, in an exposition of her work that mixed appreciation with a degree of skepticism. Specifically, he was unconvinced by her identification of the Kilburn of the early twelfth century as the place and date of origin, emphasizing considerations that Hope herself had acknowledged but not answered. He pointed to a reference to Saint Ælred of Riveaux, though the saint in question was not canonized until 1191, too late for the proposed date, and thirteen citations from Saint Bernard of Clairvaux, which Chambers thought particularly damning, since, he insisted, the references were in fact "from the Bernardine literature of the generation succeeding the saint's death" (p. 18), which meant that the date of composition would have to be put even later than the date of Saint Bernard's death, in 1153. Chambers acknowledged that scribal intervention could account for some of what troubled him but was inclined to think that the Bernardine passages were too deeply imbedded in the text to be simply explained away as scribal contamination, an observation that subsequent scholarship has confirmed. He admitted the possibility of "what the Germans would call an *Ur-Ancrene-Riwle*, which is now lost, but which may have been written for three Kilburn recluses by Godwin their 'master,'" but felt compelled to insist that such a version "is pure hypothesis" (p. 21). Still, he insisted that Hope Allen's work on the text had lasting value, even if her Kilburn identification was finally rejected, as it has been. "Miss Allen has linked up the *Ancrene Riwle* with the religious movements of the twelfth century," he wrote, "and shown it as the work of a man living at a time of many strong religious influences, sensitive to all, but not giving the zeal of a partisan to any" (p. 22). He could as easily have been talking not about the anonymous author in question but about Hope Allen herself, who, as I shall show in the next chapter, was about to set the seal on her professional career.

3

LONDON

F ollowing her return to Britain in 1920, Hope became engaged in the most professionally demanding period of her career. In this chapter I shall treat the world in which she moved, and some of the people who comprised it.

With the appearance of her articles on the *Ancrene Riwle*, Hope found herself an established scholar. The United States had joined the war, and she worked briefly as a Red Cross volunteer in Oneida. But Europe, and particularly England, was much on her mind. Transatlantic travel was impossible, at least for the moment, so she again took up certain of her American academic friends and acquaintances, to tell them what she was about and to seek their advice.

These were early days yet for Middle English studies, and the nineteenth-century habit of identifying medieval English culture with a few great names (*Beowulf*, Chaucer, Malory) who were thought to have stood against the general cultural failure, was still current. A few more searching scholars were willing to admit others to the list (Dunbar, Skelton, even Langland) but the idea that the student of literature should be concerned with the larger intellectual associations of the period was just beginning. Disciplines were separated with some severity. Anglo-Norman studies were relatively few, and even medieval Latin, the single most important cultural connection of the period, fell into no particular orbit, though some Continental scholars, mostly members of religious orders, pursued the sorts of texts that continued to receive Hope's attention. But there was, too, a lingering suspicion in England, of all things medieval, which not even Ruskin and the Gothic revival could disguise. Apart from a few great minds, things were different in those days, and decidedly un-British. Thank God for the Reformation! Against such prejudice stood a natural interest in English literature and English history, and it was to this interest that Hope and her generation appealed, dismissing William Morris, Romantic adulation and the rest. No facet of a nation's past is without interest; English literature did not really begin with Shakespeare. And from these givens, much could be made to follow.

In 1917, Hope had written to Carleton Brown (among others), now teaching at the University of Minnesota, concerning her work on the *Ancrene Riwle*, and to him she confessed some unease at the early date she was going to assign it. He wrote back on May 15 (the letter is at Bryn Mawr), encouraging her to go ahead: "I don't think you need to be disturbed by the early date. . . . All our information hitherto in regard to this document is purely tentative. It would be great good fortune if we could find some solid external facts on which to ground our theories." On October 12 she wrote to her advisor on liturgical matters, Father Walter Frere, inquiring about some liturgical points. He replied on November 3, reporting, among other things, his own difficulties with the early date she proposed and insisting that the "general character of the sources seems to me to point rather to the thirteenth century." Hope replied on November 22, arguing that "if I can get circumstantial evidence of an historical nature putting the work in the early twelfth century, which is sufficiently strong, then I can hope that it will force into line the questions of language and liturgy. If so, the results of the investigation will be all the more interesting." In subsequent correspondence, in particular in a letter of July 11, 1918, Frere continued to express his doubts, as did Professor Craigie, in a letter written on Christmas Day, 1918. But once she had committed herself in print, Hope did not retreat, and for the next thirty years she was all but inflexible.

Her work, however, did not pass unchallenged. The Reverend Vincent McNabb, O.P., an energetic and popular Dominican priest well known for his argumentative but humane sermons and for his Hyde Park oratory, and an energetic defender of his order, printed in the *Modern Language Review* for 1916 an article arguing, rather against the evidence, that the work was Dominican in origin, and that Hope's early-twelfth-century date was therefore mistaken. Wrong on his first point, he was, as it happened, right on his second, and he returned to his theme in 1926 in the *Review of English Studies*, publishing two short answers in the same journal. In all of this Hope was not much taken with the tone of McNabb's address, and there is a letter from the editor of *Modern Language Review* in 1916, in answer to one from her, explaining his reasons for allowing the publication of McNabb's first article. But at length McNabb himself came under attack. His 1926 pieces were in response to Chambers' article on recent *Ancrene Riwle* scholarship, and they caused his argument to be taken up both by Chambers and by a very able Jesuit scholar, the Reverend Herbert Thurston, S.J. Argument and counterargument continued, and McNabb's reasoning, based primarily on liturgical evidence, was effectively disposed of by two attacks. The second of these by Thurston was astonishingly severe, all but charging McNabb with dishonesty. Hope later recorded her satisfaction that the answer had come from McNabb's "co-religionist" so that she herself could not be charged with having taken a "partisan position." But the extraordinary severity of Thurston's attack is remarkable even now, directed as it was against an evangelical preacher who had rather unknowingly ventured into an academic arena. Less than five years before her death, and after a gap of more than thirty years, Hope and McNabb exchanged letters in what was in effect a very courteous farewell. Her relationship with Thurston remained correct but formal.

The war ended late in 1918, and Hope's desire to return to England quickened. On July 7, 1920, her last close tie to Oneida was cut: her father died, leaving her not only free to travel again but with the means to do so. Certain stocks in Oneida Community, Ltd., came to her, just as her now-married brother assumed the presidency of the company. Throughout the next two decades he was available to advise her on her investments, but Hope took a keen and informed interest in her shares and always understood how far she could reasonably extend herself. She did what she could to settle her affairs and left for England before the end of 1920.

It is worth considering what Hope Allen found when she returned, after an eight-year lapse, to the nation she unfailingly called England. She would not have forgotten what Henry James had called "the rich, humanized landscape," or the libraries that housed the manuscripts of Richard Rolle with which she was concerned. Most of what she remembered from Cambridge impressions would have been confirmed, even in London, even after the war. Britain often strikes American visitors, at least initially, as more compact, more connected, more coherent, than the energetic, rather inchoate nation they have just left. Newspapers, the class system, and, after 1922, the radio all contributed to this comforting illusion. The courteous regard accorded a woman scholar would have impressed her as well. But there were other factors at work too, some conditioned by the recent war, others by social attitudes posing as culture.

Internationally, both the British people and their government were for the moment more concerned with a past enemy, Germany, and a political enemy, France, than with the United States. At the Paris Peace Conference in 1919, and into the early 1920s, France was intent on imposing as high a reparations settlement as possible on Germany, whose industrial future she feared. The English, in the person of Lloyd George, were concerned to restrain the French, both to create in Germany a marketplace for English goods and also to prevent French industrial domination on the Continent. After 1923 the American Dawes Plan, urged on by a 40 percent fall in the French franc, sought to effect a balanced budget, stabilized currency, and reparation by the ingenious method of leaving reparation funds in Germany, so that France and England would obtain German goods, not German capital. The plan was a spur to German industry of the first order and, in practice, tied American interests to German repayment and to stability, which meant to peace.

But if American and British interests stood against French in some respects, in others they did not. The American tariff of 1922 all but eliminated restrictions on raw materials, which poured into American markets, a practice which had benefits for Latin America and Asia, but not for Europe. Early in 1921 the British ambassador to the United States wrote:

> The central ambition of the realist school of American politicians is to win for America the position of leading nation in the world and also leader among the English-speaking nations. To do this they intend to have the strongest navy and the largest mercantile marine. They intend also to prevent us from paying our debt by sending goods to America, and they look for the opportunity to treat us as a vassal state so long as the debt remains unpaid.

American cultural attitudes toward Europe in general and Britain in particular were in the 1920s and 1930s what they remain today, complex and contradictory, defensively admiring. Those relatively few Americans, and fewer still women, who had the advantage, not to say luxury, of a university education would have been likely to point to London as the center of what they would have confidently called civilization. There was a moral as well as a value judgment lurking in the designation. As a city London was thought to lack the more notorious aspects of Paris and to be, on the whole, better kept than, and without the papist associations of, Rome. Madrid was rather beyond the American pale; Berlin had, by the war, eliminated itself from serious consideration. The north of Europe was too cold, and was not the east Slavic? No; for an American of the "right" class and economic position, London stood at the apex of European, and so of human, culture. If Paris was, as Oscar Wilde remarked, where good Americans went when they died, London was the more respectable choice for their moral but still breathing bodies.

Against these larger cultural perceptions, it is difficult to know, but less difficult to guess, what more personal perceptions attracted Hope Allen to England. She came, after all, from three environments: Oneida, Bryn Mawr, and Harvard. Each of them had much to recommend it, but each she would have found limiting as well.

From Oneida she had gained much: familial trust and support, but also an awareness of her own considerable intellectual powers. These talents, family, friends, and school had encouraged and so propelled her into the wider world of intellect that Bryn Mawr had come to represent. Yet in each environment it is probable that she felt a touch (perhaps more than a touch), of provinciality and a sense that there were other questions to be asked and other places to ask them in. If that was what brought her to Radcliffe, it was not enough to hold her there, and the promise of that other Cambridge, glimpsed in her 1910 travels, proved more attractive.

The attraction of England for her was twofold: it gave her an awareness that the self which from adolescence had been hers could be acknowledged, respected, left intact, even while, as at Oneida and at Bryn Mawr, it was drawn into intimate association with like-minded and personally sympathetic scholars. To be an American living in England in the 1920s and 1930s carried with it a position in society that was also outside of society. For one thing, the class system, less pronounced in academic circles than outside them, did not seem to apply to her, at least not as it did to others. An American was not English, or even British, or from the empire either. But she was not quite a foreigner; it was not as if she came from France. From all of this Hope Allen derived a sense of respect for her interests and herself and an acceptance of these qualities with no imperative to conform to any requirements other than academic ones. Added to this was the fact that her gender did not seem to inhibit scholarly communication, a circumstance which did not obtain in the United States of America. The great attraction that England held for her was both personal and social. It represented a degree of personal and academic freedom she had not known before, and that engaged her deeply.

To understand her circumstances it is necessary to recall the ways in which locality bore in on the individual in early twentieth-century America. It was only in the 1920s, after all, that more Americans came to live in cities than in the country, though since a city was, by American definition, a community of more than twenty-five hundred persons, the nation was hardly urban, nor was Oneida a metropolis even by that generous description. But the climate in city and country alike was hardly pastoral. Local traditions and narrow, not to say provincial, customs were everywhere apparent, and not infrequently confirmed by law. Depending on place and circumstance, these customs could include racism of the most brutal and violent kind; the limitation, in all but a few exceptional cases, of higher education to white males; a financial status quo which, while open by European standards, still restricted the fruits of its production to upper- and middle-class whites.

But there was another side to American society, and it was equally apparent. For the worker, man and woman, was better protected in America than he was soon to become on the Continent and than he had been throughout most of the nineteenth century. The 1920s would end in financial chaos, but the image of American middle-class prosperity, which is now understood to have been limited to a rather narrow portion of the population, was perceived as having become general. Things were safe, it seemed, people and money, and they could do what they liked with it, within reason.

True enough, there were those too for whom the 1920s were, as F. Scott Fitzgerald said, the "Jazz Age." But they were a tiny part of the population and by then had moved, for the most part, to Paris. They did not become an important fact of cultural life until late in the decade, and then mainly to college students (at least to those interested in modern literature) and to intellectuals. Back home things were different. Local custom mattered. For the rich, America was indeed the land of liberty, if not of license; for others life was more circumscribed, convention more absolute. It was not until 1961, the year after Hope Allen's death, that the Supreme Court established the rights of an indigent man to a lawyer and to adequate representation in court. But in England money went further, the individual was accorded more respect, and gender, at least for a foreigner, was less decisive.

The defense of British institutions implied in Hope Allen's letter to the *Times* on the relative merits of Radcliffe, Harvard, and Newnham is typical of her respect for the established order, as is her American irritation at seeing it wantonly attacked. A related story among her Oxford papers may help illustrate the point. At some point in the 1930s, a friend, Joan Wake, took Hope Allen to a meeting of the London club called "The Set of Odd Volumes" to hear, as she thought, an entertaining after-dinner speaker. The chat included a reference to oysters, and an aside by the speaker that, since biology had declared them to be bisexual, he wondered "which cloak-room" they chose. The rather feeble joke, hardly risqué by modern standards, was perhaps not very daring even when Hope Allen heard it, but she was not amused. Perhaps in other circumstances she would have been less unbending, but the circumstance struck her as an inappropriate forum for such reference; the after-dinner idiom was evidently new to her. She seems to have had the sense too that it was a pity to see a Briton lessen the ceremony of a London dinner, and this same sense shows itself in the seriousness of mind she brought to the academic institutions that were a part of her daily life. No doubt there were unmistakably American attitudes present in all of this: a sense of the effect individual attack could have; an awareness of the value of institutions as a means of projecting reason, unanimity, and order; all values attractive to a woman who might feel that local custom could operate against the individual, particularly one whose gender had placed her in an academic minority. There may also have been a sense of the fragility of institutions, and their impermanence, evident to one who was much concerned with medieval tradition. There may also have been present something of the American fascination with English antiquity and a certain lack of sophistication. Whatever the cause, her interest in stability, in a present linked to its past, guided many of her attachments at this time.

During her years in London throughout the next two decades her attachments to Oneida remained strong, cultivated by correspondence with many friends, Jesse Catherine Kinsley (b. 1858) among them. This personal correspondence, selections of which were published in a 1983 edition of Kinsley's letters, shows Hope at her most relaxed and informal, concerned with the family and friends she knew and with the details of community life. It was this contact, perhaps more than any other, that sustained her during her years abroad and maintained her sense of being still a part of the Oneida community. Other friendships, with Esther Loenthal at Smith College, and Charlotte D'Evelyn at Mount Holyoke, also kept her in touch, if somewhat remotely, with American academic life, but her deepest roots were in Oneida, and those she carefully nourished.

This was the period during which her academic work in Britain took hold. On December 7, 1920, a decade after she first began working in British libraries, Hope was admitted to the Public Record Office in Chancery Lane, where for the next twenty years she would carry on her most significant work. The building was constructed in 1232 by King Henry III as a home for converted Jews on a road made by the Knights Templar to connect their old palace in Holborn with their new one, just off Fleet Street. Then as now, medieval manuscripts were read in the Round Room, a small, well-appointed reading room a fraction of the size of the similar room in the British Museum. In Hope's day a clear distinction was observed between consulting legal records, for which a charge was made, and reading literary records, for which there was none. The number of readers at the time was relatively small, and few were medievalists. Although figures on the number of readers were not reported in the early annual reports, by 1934, the Public Records Office reported a total of 9,692 visits; by 1983 the number stood at 113,555. The number of volumes inspected rose from 17,685 to 409,066 over the same period.

But if the readers were few, the quantity of materials the building contained was anything but. In spite of civil wars, fires, and periods of indifference, the national records of Britain, which date back to the eleventh century, are the best preserved in Europe, though the roll format in which many were set down does nothing to facilitate access. Yet a roll is a powerful and impressive object. Turning the folios of one of the massive Plea Rolls, or examining the names inscribed on one of the Assize Rolls, the historian is brought into intimate contact with the events he seeks to understand as he is in no other way. The effect of reading a roll is difficult to explain, but not to experience. It is as though, for a moment, the past happens again, so that justices, scribes, the accused, and the witnesses appear before you. A name on a roll embodies a person as no printed page ever can. A man or woman, dead five hundred years, suddenly springs into being, complete with the interests, the passions, the greed and the charities of the time.

Hope's initial interest was with Richard Rolle, and in seeking to trace his associations she examined the records for Yorkshire, particularly the Plea, Coram Rege, and Assize Rolls. Indeed, her first order was for three large Plea Rolls, which record civil actions at common law brought at common pleas. She was concerned to discover, among great northern families like the Scropes, the Boltons, and the Daltons what the sources for Richard Rolle's support might have been, and in 1924 in the Assize Rolls she had success, discovering, for example, Henry le Scrope's association on August 18, 1324, with the Yorkshire trial of Robert Wawayn and others, who, though the king's bailiffs, had oppressed the people under them. On June 12, 1324, a Patent Roll written in Westminster records the original commission on which the justices acted.

In an unconnected reference, fifty-eight years later, Geoffrey le Scrope recorded a bequest of 20 shillings to an anchoress at Hampole (perhaps Richard Rolle's disciple Margaret de Kirkeby, Hope estimated) and, put together with a hundred other references, such entries built up a picture of the northern community, at once very powerful and very devout, within which Rolle, his followers, and his devotions flourished.

The examination of public documents, both in London and in county archives, is no easy, and no quick, matter. In her work Hope screened rolls, looking for references under Yorkshire ("Ebor:" the Latin abbreviation for Yorkshire, written prominently in the margins facilitated the first stage) to find allusions to Richard Rolle, or to those associated with him, or, no doubt, to any recluses who might be mentioned. A Coram Rege roll could treat Saint Mary's, the great Benedictine abbey in York with which Rolle or his patrons might have business; a roll treating King Edward III's sister Eleanor traveling to her marriage in 1332 alluded to an anchoress enclosed by Algate. Each allusion which is confidently, even proudly, recovered is paid for by hours spent in unavailing research, and the pattern which emerges is always subject to revision. Fascinated by genealogy since childhood, Hope may have owed her later interest in the early ownership of medieval manuscripts as much to her work in the Public Record Office as to anything else. In any event, only after she began working regularly in public documents did the interest really take hold, transforming her studies on the *Ancrene Riwle*.

Her return to Britain was greatly facilitated by her Cambridge friend Marietta Pallis, who had bought a house in Cheyne Row, in which she invited Hope to lodge. Hope accepted, and the attachment begun at Newnham and sustained during the war by correspondence continued. But in the years between Hope's sojourn at Newnham and her return in 1920, Marietta had herself changed direction. Her present occupation now was primarily that of a painter of landscapes and portraits, and the house she had acquired was only a few doors from one formerly owned by J. M. W. Turner. Marietta was in many ways an ideal landlady, unconventional to the point of eccentricity but undemanding and willing to leave Hope to herself; most of Hope's guests had no idea how close she and her landlady were, and few even met her. Hope paid for her lodging, which was on the top floor, her position of choice both in her London and in her Oneida apartments. In the 1930s Hope bought a half-share in the house but sold it back to Marietta (perhaps with the offer of resale after the war) when she returned to America in 1939. After 1921, 116 Cheyne Walk, SW 10 was her London address.

In some ways the house was ideal, combining local familiarity with national associations. Not far away, at No. 4, George Eliot had died in 1880, a year before Thomas Carlyle in nearby Cheyne Row. Whistler had lived at No. 96, Turner at No. 119. In Hope's own day other artists were or had been active: the sculptor John Tweed at No. 108, Philip Wilson Steer at No. 109. Marietta was keeping good company.

Affecting that she still owned a share of the building, Hope described the house to a Mr. Gilday in a letter dated February 25, 1943, now in the Bodleian Library, Oxford:

I stay when in England at a little made-over workman's house at the shabby end (and) where the river has not been embanked the street is narrow. The lime trees come into the upper landscape from the windows, and below as many as 20 swans sometimes swim about in the blue-silvery water – with the church where Blake was married across the river, its bells clanging out from time to time – and the flour mills still keeping in their group, the peaked malt houses of Bolingbroke's manor house where Pope wrote the *Essay on Man*. I own a share of this little house which is the home of an English college friend of Greek blood who also owns adjoining cottages and a paved yard at the back, from which in war she can send lovely pressed flowers (the air now being pure).

The houses today (115 and 116 have been joined together) are a story higher, and have been tastefully redecorated by their present owner. The downstairs restaurant that was in operation during Hope's residence has disappeared, leaving only attractive high ceilings to mark its former existence, but the house is still very much what Hope recalled, and its charm still exists. The malt houses she mentions have also disappeared, but the church in which Blake was married, Battersea Parish Church of Saint Mary's, still dominates the far side of the river and has indeed the associations Hope recalled, together with one other she did not: Benedict Arnold is buried in the crypt. The sunset is less vivid from the Chelsea side of the river than from Wandsworth, where Saint Mary's stands, so it was to Saint Mary's that J. M. W. Turner would go to paint the sun setting into the river and to observe cloud formations from the oriel vestry window. The church itself is the most salient feature of the view from Hope's window.

Then as now Cheyne Walk looked in two directions, back toward the substantial homes and institutions of Chelsea and Victoria: the Royal Hospital, Chelsea, is a short distance away, as is the Chelsea Physic Garden, founded in 1673, while downriver lies the working-class area surrounding Chelsea Wharf, today dominated by the Gas Works, the Lots Road pumping station, and a London Underground generating station, but embracing too a boys' school, now the Heatherly School of Art, an adventure playground, and a thin trickle of antique shops that seem to have seeped down from King's Road. The area has now become a contained and active community, connected to rich Chelsea by financial ties but maintaining its own rough identity. Its gentrification is by no means as far advanced as is Cheyne Row's, and the area between Lots

Road and King's Road gives a good sense of what the streets just below No. 116 would have been like in the 1920s and 1930s.

One Cheyne Walk association that Hope maintained was Crosby Hall, originally constructed as Sir John Crosby's banqueting hall in the late Middle Ages, subsequently owned by Thomas More, and now a hall or residence containing a refectory and a library for women graduates opened in 1927. She would sometimes take her evening meal there, and it was there she met Mabel Day to discuss her difficult collaboration on the *Book of Margery Kempe*. But the part of Chelsea in which Hope took up residence, rough and unfashionable though it may have been in some eyes, suited her very well. Unlike the more refined parts of Cambridge and London she had known earlier, it enforced few social distinctions and was relatively "open" to an unattached and independent American woman and to a somewhat bohemian (if property-owning) artist. It was a good place to work. It was an even better place to live.

Between 1921 and 1939 Hope and Marietta were drawn together not only by their Cambridge past but also by shared artistic aspiration, painting for Marietta (who had now put poetry aside), fiction for Hope. In a letter of March 17, 1949 to Mabel Day now in Oxford Hope wrote:

> I left Bryn Mawr in 1906 with the intention to continue if I could the sort of literary writing for which I had got the essay prize in my class. There (under the eye of Henry James who was our graduation speaker) I was too self-conscious to go on with writing, and since I had to earn my living, went on to research—fortunately on a writer who took my fancy as a real personality—rare among medieval theological authors. But I always kept at the back of my mind a project of one literary writing or another. In an interval at Hickling in 1922 I sent to the Atlantic Monthly a story based on the continual talk of the wonderful old woman to whose home (then in a mill on the marshes) Miss Pallis had taken me in June 1911. The story was instantly accepted and another asked for. That winter the rag yard behind 116 Cheyne Walk was reclaimed and my lodgings disturbed. I wrote two similar tales then, of which I sent you the last—written in 1924. I am always very diffuse in literary writing at first, and revise endlessly.

Evidently there were other stories too. The same letter reports, "In the depression I tried . . . to get one or two Norfolk stories printed," and notes that Mrs. Gibbs, Hope's Norfolk informant, died on April 1, 1940, aged ninety, "saying the last years she prayed for me everyday wherever I was." But since 1934, Hope insisted, she had set all her creative literary work aside.

Hope's account may have been based on her best memory at the time, but there is reason to doubt it. Not only did she write stories at Bryn Mawr, but among the family papers in Oneida is an undated letter that mentions two others, "Unearned Increment" and "A Strain of Persian," which I have not been able to trace.

The three stories she did publish, two in the *Atlantic Monthly* for February and September, 1923, and one in the *Dial* for December, 1927, all reflect the Norfolk background she shared with Marietta Pallis, whose tiny cottage, "Long Gores," near Hickling, Norwich, was her second home in England, and the center for her and Marietta's first excursions into the Norfolk countryside. In the first of Hope's *Atlantic* stories, "Ancient Grief," the protagonist is John Williams, "a young American who had dabbled in literature during the year since he had left college," and who returns to his ancestral home in Norfolk to learn, among other things, of his grandmother's lost love, and of his own origins, which rather diminish his self-confidence.

In the second story, "A Glut of Fruit," an entire family returns to the father's East Anglian home, where the daughter, over her father's objections, falls in love with a local. In each story it is the characterization as much as the plot that commands attention. Thus in "Ancient Grief" John Williams' landlady is described as a "squat woman of swarthy skin and jetty hair," and he is told that such "were remnants . . . of a primitive race cut off by the fens; and he saw also many tall fair ones, descendants of Norse invaders who had landed on this coast. The rise and fall of speech of all of them went to the same haunting tune." The "glut of fruit" of the title refers both to the fruit trees in bloom by the cottage where the family stays and to the number of able young men who leave for America, there not being employment for them at home.

By far the most ambitious of Hope's stories was "The Fanciful Countryman," which appeared in the Christmas 1927 *Dial*. It concerns the life of an East Anglian working man, Billie Appleyard, and his youthful dissatisfaction with life in the country, his abortive move into service in London, and his return to the East Anglian countryside of his birth, where he finds fulfillment and love. The length and complexity of the narrative go beyond anything Hope had attempted before, as does the Norfolk dialect she maintained throughout.

> "He fare extra sharp," said his mother the Sunday evening after he had left for London. "See how Billa got on however he torn. . . . He's sharp at that work. It's a rum job he can't be a bit sharper and see what's gain. Whatever make him that onesa? He's the masterest boy for a change I ever did see. He look different from the rest and he fare different."

Billie has "an extra sense, his fancy," that drives him, and throughout the story Hope shows a sensitivity to the way the class system, both that of London and that of servants' hall, can impinge on a sensitive and able young workingman from the country. Her knowledge of the East Anglian background of the story came not from Mrs. Gibbs but from a number of young women servants whom Hope and Marietta befriended during the time they spent in Norfolk. Some of these young women they assisted financially, and among the family papers in Oneida are letters of thanks from two in particular. Hope and Marietta thus knew the Norfolk countryside in some depth, and Hope's love of the countryside that began in the American Adirondacks thus continued in the East Anglian fens.

Back in London, Hope took charge of things at No. 116 when Marietta was away. The family papers also preserve a letter of July 6, 1926, to Mrs. Fleming, who lived at No. 118, insisting that her workmen had been responsible for damage to the roof at No. 116 (the bathroom roof leaked after a rain), and that Mrs. Fleming's cat, Georgie, had befriended the cat from the eating house, to the detriment of the garden. There were few aspects of English life that Hope did not engage during this decade.

During this period too Hope often wrote for, or at least to, the popular press; some of her letters remain unpublished. Not long after her unpublished letter in defense of women at Cambridge, on November 16, 1926, the *Times* printed her reply to an article that had incautiously remarked that the Latin prayer "O Bone Jesu" was not from a known liturgical source. In her reply, one of the few times she anticipated a longer study (which never appeared) with a shorter one, Hope noted the background to the prayer but thought it little more than a recension of the last part of the second meditation of Saint Anselm, with some additions. She remarked:

The devotion to the holy name of Jesus was a highly significant and attractive feature of the late medieval religious history of England. Richard Rolle had a romantic part in launching the cult, but after his day it touched movements of general European scope and, though usually initiated by mystics, in the end permeated general English popular devotion. The prayer "O Bone Jesu" was a favorite of the cult, and was itself a significant landmark in English religious history.

One of her earliest professional associates now became her collabora-tor. In a letter to Mabel Day of June 12, 1946, Hope records her impression of John Alexander Herbert, of the British Museum, remarking that

> he is a wonderful man but in some curious ways child-like, and during the years when I was said to have better luck in getting work out of him than anyone, found a prime factor was paying him in small bits – his wife told me he was one to save 6 pence and give away 5 pounds – and I saw this was true. He refused large jobs from Sotheby's but did what amounted to almost weekly work.

Childlike he may have been, but it is difficult to overstate the assistance Hope derived from him. Not only did Herbert point out, examine, and index whole manuscripts for her, but both of her volumes on Rolle owe much to his efforts. Herbert worked carefully over the entire text of her great volume *Writings Ascribed to Richard Rolle, Hermit of Hampole, and Materials for His Biography*, and the final proof went to press from his correcting hand. Hope rightly reported that Herbert's "learning and accuracy have been constantly at my disposal. Wherever possible he has gone over the quotations from unedited works with rotographs of the manuscripts, and he has several times read the whole book in manuscript and in proof." In a letter dated December 11, 1927 (now at Bryn Mawr), Herbert informed her that he had at last sent her volume to press and congratulated her "most heartily upon this great achievement, a perma-nent & very substantial contribution to knowledge."

Another close friendship that Hope developed in the 1920s was with the Oxford don Dorothy Everett, with whom she worked as an equal. Although the British convention did not allow the use of first names in correspondence until the 1950s, the friendship was no doubt deepened by mutual interests. In the *Modern Language Review* for 1922 and 1923, Everett published a long article, "The Middle English Prose *Psalter* of Richard Rolle of Hampole," to which Hope contributed, and the two took tea together when they met at the British Museum. In later years Everett told a story connected with one of those meetings, recounting that once when they were at table in a London tea shop the serving of their tea was much delayed. Hope, according to her custom, was talking rapidly and seemed not to have noticed, but then all at once she reached over to a neighboring table, removed the teapot, filled both their cups, and then replaced the pot without breaking the flow of her conversation. However eccentric the incident may have seemed to her friend, no doubt for her it was as though for a moment she was back in the community dining room in the Oneida Mansion House, sharing food and drink. England had become familiar to her.

During the 1920s she also made the acquaintance of a number of Continental scholars who were working in related areas, including a good number of Roman Catholic clergymen. It was during this decade that she began to steer a middle course between British scholars, including the markedly anti-Catholic G. G. Coulton, and Continental ones, most of whom were Catholic, many in orders. My own impression is that, as the years progressed, she became drawn intellectually toward the Catholic scholars, though she was always careful to maintain her British friendships intact. Her correspondence with all was varied, and, though mutually rewarding (Hope usually gave as much help as she got), with certain clerics it was particularly detailed. In her printed acknowledgments to her study of Rolle she lists some of these: The Prefect of the Vatican Library, who had granted her admission, the first woman so admitted, she believed; the Benedictine scholar Dom Maurice Noetinger, O.S.B., of Solesmes, with whom she had in fact several points of difference but with whom she conducted a learned correspondence; and the Reverend Paul Grossjean, S.J., one of the Bollandists whose accuracy in historical detail she much admired. Among these colleagues two stand out in particular, one for the closeness of the collaboration, the other for the more abstract quality of personal esteem.

Hope's correspondence with the Franciscan teacher, scholar, and paleographer P. (for Pater) Livarius Oliger, O.F.M., was one of the most rewarding of her career. She had been introduced to Oliger by A. G.

Little, twenty years her senior and well known both in London and in Rome as the founder of the British Society of Franciscan Studies, whose publications had, since 1907, put British Franciscan scholarship on a new footing. Little had taken a first class degree in modern history at Oxford in 1886 and would add to it an honorary D.Litt. in 1928. He had studied in Germany, and had held a professorship in history at University College, Cardiff, which he had resigned in 1901, but not before he had made a substantial contribution toward establishing the history curriculum at the new University of Wales. He had subsequently taught history at Manchester, continued his numerous publications on Franciscan history, and acted as a contributing editor for the *Dictionary of National Biography* and the *Victoria County History*. From these and other professional associations he acquired a wide range of friends and acquaintances whom he encouraged in Franciscan studies from his house in Sevenoaks, and he was an obvious point of reference for a young American scholar seeking assistance on a Franciscan topic or with the Vatican Library. Seeking Rolle manuscripts in Italy, Hope took Little's introduction to Oliger not only as a way of gaining entry to Italian libraries but also, as it transpired, as an introduction to paleography.

Oliger, who was to introduce her to these mysteries, was born in Schorbach in 1875 and ordained in 1900. He was known for his distinguished studies of Franciscan history that appeared regularly in the journals *Antonianum* and *Archivum Franciscanum Historicum*, both of which commemorated his work in 1951 with long obituaries. Hope later credited him with having pointed out a number of Rolle manuscripts in Trier and Naples, and in his office as professor of history in the College of Saint Anthony in Rome, he taught her, during an early visit, much about paleography. But as time went on her work fed his. In investigating the possibility that Rolle had written the *Regula heremitarum*, a contemporary rule for hermits, Hope approached Oliger for an opinion about the work's possible connection to the Franciscans and about its orthodoxy. About the latter he had no doubt, but he rejected the former, pointing out that the work was without a trace of Italian but, with Hope's encouragement, agreeing to undertake a study, which appeared in *Antonianum* in 1928.

Subsequent letters were particularly cordial. In 1934, having returned to the work on hermits, Oliger wrote on February 27, "It looks almost as if you were my research agency!" But the same letter (now at Bryn Mawr) also takes up a point that had irritated Hope, his reference to the Trinity College manuscript of the *Dublin Rule* as having been written in the thirteenth century, so undermining the early twelfth-century date that Hope still wished to attach to the *Ancrene Riwle*, which the less sophisticated *Dublin Rule* had followed. In his correspondence, Hope believed, Oliger, whom she had become accustomed to consult on matters of paleography, had allowed for an earlier date, but now in print he had fixed one that made her quotation of his letter "seem curious, and not very trustworthy. I certainly understood you to mean that a different date for the A.R. would change that of the Dublin rule," she remonstrated on January 2, 1934.

Such difficulties ("in my letter I spoke *conditionally*" Oliger replied) are not uncommon among scholars who work on closely related areas, but Hope required of her correspondents a fidelity to expressed opinion that few were willing to grant. In some respects her attitudes toward authority were a shade too accommodating and allowed too little room for doubt and revision. Once the matter was settled, that was that.

There is, however, a family story that may apply. According to it, one of Hope's closest and oldest clerical correspondents (the remembered description of his habit would suggest Oliger) is reported to have written to her from his deathbed asking, after all their years of academic exchange, what her religious opinions might be. Hope had none that would comfort him but was reluctant to write under such circumstances. Distressed by the question but unwilling, indeed unable, to lie, she delayed answering until he died.

If the story is true (I have found no such letter), if the priest in question was Oliger, then the story sets a certain mark on the relationship, correct and friendly, courteous and controlled, but not close in any personal sense. There was one friendship, however, where I believe Hope's academic judgment shaded over into an appreciation that was, in part, devout, and that was conveyed in her exchanges with a French Benedictine scholar of great distinction, Dom André Wilmart, O.S.B.

Dom Wilmart was unusual among French medievalists in maintaining friendships with several English medievalists, particularly in Oxford, and in exploring, from Saint Michael's Abbey at Farnborough, the manuscripts in the British Museum. Born in Orleans in 1876, Dom Wilmart graduated from the Sorbonne at nineteen, and continued at the École des Hautes Études. In 1897, already an academic of some distinction, he entered the seminary at Saint Sulpice, in Paris, but thereafter became a Benedictine and two years later, on June 24, 1899, made his profession at the Abbey of Solesmes. The following year he began his scholarly career when he edited what was believed to be a Latin translation of eighteen sermons of Origen (but which was in fact the work of Gregory of Elvire, a fourth-century Spanish bishop), *Tractatus origenis de libris ss. scripturarum*, which he published with Monsignor Peter Batiffol, who had made the identification.

But those were bad times for the Abbey of Solesmes, and indeed for the Benedictine order in France. In the wake of the Dreyfus affair a new republican government had come to power, confident that religion was a thing of the past and confirmed in the belief that it enjoyed a mandate, thanks to the anti-Dreyfus and anti-Semitic attitudes of many French Catholics, to do away with ecclesiastical power, both by abridging the influence of a traditionally conservative parochial school system and by limiting the affluence of religious congregations. Premier Pierre Waldeck-Rousseau promulgated a law that, when enforced with severity by his successor, Justin Louis Combes (a former seminarian) led to the dissolution of 17,000 "unauthorized" congregations in three months, the ancient foundation of Solesmes among them. In 1901 the monks from Solesmes took refuge in Quarr Abbey, on the Isle of Wight, and Dom Wilmart remained there until June, 1906, when, in the interests of his scholarship and supported by his superiors, he transferred to Saint Michael's Abbey, Farnborough, Hampshire.

Saint Michael's had its own story, having been built by Empress Eugénie of France, consort of Napoleon III, who had gone to England following the 1870 revolution. She bought an estate on Farnborough Hill in 1881 and lived there (with occasional trips to her native Spain) until her death in 1920 at the age of ninety-four. The year before Dom Wilmart arrived at Farnborough, a law separating church and state had been promulgated in France, and some of the earlier animosities had lessened. But it was not until 1920, after the first World War (during which Dom Wilmart returned to France to offer his services) that monks from the Abbey of Solesmes were allowed to return, and by then Dom Wilmart was established at Saint Michael's. From 1917 to 1919 he was posted to

London, assigned to the French military mission which was attached to the war office. His friendship with the British scholar Kenneth Sisam and his close knowledge of British Museum manuscripts dates from these years, when he took care also to keep his scholarship in good repair. From 1919 until 1928 he remained at Saint Michael's, producing his own canon of learned and discriminating articles, for which he made frequent visits to London, Oxford, and the Continent. It was during this period that Hope made his acquaintance, through a meeting at the British Museum.

Intellectually he gradually moved away from liturgical and historical studies (in which, however, he retained a lifelong interest), to the study of medieval spirituality, a shift precipitated by his work on the canon of Saint Anselm's prayers, where his remarkable knowledge of monastic manuscripts made him expert in identifying, understanding, and explaining traditions of devotion that had been all but lost. Called to the Vatican in 1929 to catalogue the Latin manuscripts of Queen Christina of Sweden, the *Reginenses latini*, he remained a monk of Saint Michael's Abbey, to which he was making his way when the outbreak of World War II caught him in Paris. He died there in April 1941, having spent his last days examining manuscripts.

Dom Wilmart's bibliography contains almost four hundred articles, many of which relate directly to English medieval devotion, and he seems to have had personal and spiritual qualities that impressed themselves on many who knew him. Years after his death, Kenneth Sisam, a learned and practical New Zealander, wrote to Hope with rare sympathy of the personal loss he still felt in Dom Wilmart's death. It is not too much to say that Hope cultivated the distinguished Benedictine as she did no other scholar, although she once confessed to Oliger, who had met Wilmart, that she was "a little uncertain sometimes about his understanding me since most of his international friends talk French with him. But the great difficulty is his deafness—I can never be perfectly sure that he is hearing." But Hope (whose French was not without accent) took the trouble to obtain copies of manuscripts of a life of Saint Christiana and the "Epistle of Eva," which suggests something of the nature of their friendship, which comes very clear in their correspondence. In the course of their exchange, Wilmart turns, by 1933, from English to French, though sometimes sending a postcard in English. Throughout, the tone is correct and courteous, but it is also relaxed and sometimes informal. Like Hope's correspondence with Paul Grossjean, S.J., and with Wilmart's fraternal colleague Louis Gougaud, O.S.B., both distinguished medieval historians and students of spirituality, it is concerned largely with academic matters, questions of manuscript location, ownership, and access; patristic and other allusions; and more general problems of textual interpretation, as well as matters relating to publication. But unlike her correspondence with other priests, it is familiar, even occasionally unguarded, and communicates a respect born of deep knowledge both of their mutual problems and of the manuscripts on which their work rested.

In matters relating to Richard Rolle, on whom Wilmart himself would also publish, he treats Hope with utmost respect, though he was somewhat more guarded on the *Ancrene Riwle* (he distrusted Hope's early date). Still, he was able to record a shock at finding an unexpected manuscript, while asking for information about its owner. As was appropriate to his calling, Wilmart kept a certain distance from the unmarried woman who was his colleague and friend, and if they did not exchange pious reflections on the nature of the texts to which they had dedicated themselves, they enjoyed the familiarity of scholars who understood a mutual interest and entertained the utmost confidence in each other's learning and ability. Prudence, short library hours, and the distance Wilmart had to travel to London meant that their meetings, conversations, and occasional lunches were limited for the most part to the British Museum, but it was from these contacts that their friendship sprang.

For her part, Hope may not have recorded Wilmart's private opinion in print as often as she did that of, for example, Herbert or Oliger, but she seems to have found in the Benedictine something deeper. A nonbeliever is sometimes better placed than someone more devout to appreciate, or even to understand, the strength and resonance of a life dedicated to religion, and amid the careful citation and precise allusion of their correspondence it is possible to catch on Hope's side a tone of respect, even of reverence, which goes beyond her customary academic formality. In an exchange with a colleague that took place more than a decade after Wilmart's death, she cited his work as a standard of correctness and offered to supply a copy of the manuscript under dispute as something she owed to his memory. She knew as collaborators, colleagues, and sometimes adversaries a number of Roman Catholic clerics; she valued none more than Dom Wilmart.

During the period of her friendship with Wilmart, there was one other religious association that moved her, and that was with Syon Abbey, in South Brent, Devon, the English Bridgittine mother house, with which she would come to associate much late-medieval spirituality. The original Syon Abbey had been founded by King Henry V in 1415 at Twickenham, not far from London, but in 1431 it had moved to Isleworth, nearby. The Bridgittine Order, otherwise known as the order of the Most Holy Saviour, had been founded by the Swedish mystic Saint Bridget (d. 1373), and each community actually consisted of two communities, one of sixty nuns, the other of thirteen priests, four deacons, and eight lay brothers. The abbess governed both communities in temporal matters, and the elected superior of the other community undertook their spiritual direction.

Protected in its early days by royal patronage, Syon flourished and rapidly acquired lands and rents which seemed to assure its continuation. Apart from its royal and noble associations, Syon was known for the ecstatic quality of the devotions it encouraged, the attention it gave to its extensive library, and the writing and publication of its members. The extent of Syon's library has been estimated from an early catalogue and from the Sacristan's Account Rolls, which have survived, but the nature of its spirituality remains a matter of discussion, though there is a tendency developing (to which Hope may have inadvertently contributed) of crediting almost all late-medieval ecstatic spirituality to Syon's influence. Such attribution has the advantage of providing learned sources for almost any devout practice, but carries with it the danger that religious attitudes will be viewed in a largely rhetorical and derivative light, and that their more erratic and human qualities will be set aside.

But whatever Syon's impact may have been, the abbey did not survive the dissolution of the monasteries. Its reputation both religious and financial made it an easy target for the reformers, and in 1534 it was suppressed, the Reverend Richard Reynolds of the abbey suffering for his belief at Tyburn. The community itself was expelled to the Continent (though recalled briefly under Queen Mary) and in 1594 settled in Lisbon, where it remained, a distinctly English order of nuns (the male community having ended in 1695), for two and a half centuries. In 1861 a combination of difficulties in Portugal and increased toleration of Catholics in England made it desirable for the order to return, which it did, though not to its former site (luxuriously appointed by Robert Adams as a seat of the Duke of Northumberland), but to a new location in South Brent, Devon. Now the longest surviving community of religious women in Britain, it is said that during all the years in Portugal only one non-British member was admitted, but a fire in Lisbon destroyed most of the community records. Syon was a long-standing community of women with a reputation not only for piety but also for learning, and it was this mixture that attracted Hope Allen.

The original impetus for her visit may have come from Coulton before the war, and her first visit was probably with Margaret Deanesly, but in April 1928, she visited Syon with Joan Wake, who was a Catholic, and it was then that she came to know the abbess, Dame Mary Teresa Jocelyn, the fifty-sixth in succession, a learned and able woman who at once impressed Hope with the seriousness of her mind and with the interest she took in Hope's work. If she remained true to form, Hope probably attempted to draw the abbess or her assistants into some kind of collaboration, particularly since various articles in Syon's publication, the *Poor Soul's Friend*, showed the community's historical interests.

I do not mean to overstate Hope's Catholic associations, whether with Oliger and Wilmart, or with Syon Abbey. Her first association in each instance was academic, and none had as marked an influence as did Coulton, the arch-anti-Catholic. But it is hard to escape the conclusion that Hope found in her Catholic colleagues a sympathy for mysticism and for the religion she studied which went beyond agreement or disagreement. One difficulty with Hope's conception of religion was that it was tied to the scholarly empiricism she brought from the study of manuscripts and historical persons, and before that at Oneida, from genealogies. But religious knowledge is not, finally, empirical, or at least is not subject to the same laws of evidence. At some intellectual level Hope undoubtedly knew that, but at another she was reluctant to accept it. She preserved a balance and continued with her work. It is to that work I shall turn in the next chapter.

4

RICHARD ROLLE

In this chapter I shall examine Hope's work on Richard Rolle, on the Vernon manuscript, and on the *Ancrene Riwle*, each of which engaged her deeply during the 1920s. In the end, she came to see that the three texts could help to illuminate some aspect of the larger issue she would by the end of the decade set herself, the examination of late-medieval religious texts. But it was not primarily with the larger issues of whatever sort that she was engaged during the 1920s. It was with Richard Rolle, and so with London libraries.

Her methods of working in libraries were as various as the institutions themselves: she wrote usually on 6-by-8-inch file cards, but also on smaller slips of paper, on scraps, in twopenny notebooks, and in small looseleaf notebooks. She recorded, folio by folio, whatever points of interest presented themselves: names of places or persons, dates and allusions to saints, to other works, occasionally to scribes, to decoration and illumination, to changes in scribes, and to anything else that caught her attention. She would quote from most of the items in the manuscript and would go back and correct her notes, noting allusions, abbreviations, or connections with other, similar manuscripts. From these notes, or sometimes from the manuscript itself, she would often make smaller slips, listing only the work in question. The work was painstaking, detailed, and calculated to be of use to her later, though she rarely developed a larger synthesis and was mainly concerned, in her work of transcription, simply to record what was in front of her. Her notes are not bare transcripitions but are slanted toward whatever drew her toward the manuscript in question. Yet her focus was detailed and accurate: she was not one to assume her conclusions.

At the British Museum she often made the acquaintance of fellow scholars, including, in the very early 1920s, one who became particularly devoted to her, Miss Joan Wake. Joan was born on February 29, 1884, a leap year, and so could insist at the age of eighty-four that she had only twenty-one birthdays. She came from an old Roman Catholic North-ampton family (her familial connections to the Norman family named Wac were well attested) which was distinguished for its military service. Two of her three older brothers served in the King's Royal Rifle Corps, one ending as a major general, the other as a major, settling in Zimbabwe, then known as Rhodesia. The third brother entered the navy and rose to the rank of admiral. An older sister was a successful trainer of gun dogs; a younger sister married and, like her brother, moved to Zimbabwe.

In such a family it was difficult to maintain academic interests, and there are indications that Joan's concerns were not highly prized. For all his liberal views, her father left her education to a governess. Because she was stout even as a child, he declined to allow her to ride, but encouraged what he believed to be interests appropriate for a woman. But the traditional pursuits of a country squire's daughter did not engage her. In 1913, tired of occupations which seemed to her transparently vapid, she settled in London and enrolled in the London School of Economics. There by good chance she met Eileen Power, who was engaged in medieval economic research. About the same time she met Sir Frank Stenton and from him learned the value of local history, adopting his belief that there was no distinction between local history and national, that one reflected the other. At the age of thirty she took up the study of Latin and began studying local history, particularly that of her native Northamptonshire. When the war broke out, other duties, primarily with a nursing associa-tion, pressed upon her. During her war-time travels she discovered how many documents still lay in country homes unattended. Following the war she became a member of the Royal Historical Society and in 1920 enlisted the help of Sir Frank and others in establishing the North-amptonshire Record Society, whose journal, *Northamptionshire Past and Present*, she edited for decades. It is not too much to say that the journal, informal but lively as few of its counterparts among county history journals are, yet serious and detailed in its articles, still owes much to Joan's founding, and perhaps something to her personality as well. She read at the British Museum in connection with her academic work, and it was there that she met Hope.

From the beginning the friendship had obvious mutual advantages, though the two women were dissimilar. Joan was a large, physically powerful woman, extroverted, even aggressively outgoing, but with a warmth and compassion which escaped few who met her. Hope, now settled in her convictions, had a strength of character which communicated itself easily, in spite of her small size. In 1924, Joan accompanied Hope to Europe, and so in Hope's words "made possible" the trip which Hope undertook to examine Richard Rolle manuscripts in Budapest, Prague, Berlin, Cracow, Ghent, Stockholm, Lund, Vadstence, and Copenhagen. With Joan she also visited Rolle's home in Yorkshire. What Hope gave in return was perhaps less tangible but no less important. After Hope's death in 1960, Joan confided to a friend in Oneida that in her early years she had been far less confident in her talents and in her work than she appeared to others. Hope had, she said, spoken to that insecurity and had given her the beginning of the confidence she had since acquired. The debt was recorded in Joan's pamphlet *How to Complete a History and Present-Day Record of Village Life* (1925), which acknowledges "many valuable suggestions" from "Miss Hope Emily Allen, M.A., of Bryn Mawr College" and contains this: "One word about accuracy. To copy inscriptions and describe objects, even to take down a story correctly, is much more difficult than it appears at first sight. By training and practice, however, the habit of accuracy can be acquired. One faithfully recorded fact is worth a hundred theories."

To Joan Wake we owe a sympathetic and reflective obituary of Hope in *Northamptionshire Past and Present*. Joan Wrote:

> Her principal characteristics in relation to her work were her scrupulous pursuit of truth, her open-mindedness, her just though charitable judgments, a rare intellectual integrity. She would hover for weeks like a hawk in mid-air over some difficult problem, discuss it with her friends, then suddenly swoop to an independent decision, which, however, if further evidence came to light she would at once reconsider.

The statement shows what it is easy to forget: the degree of imagination needed to arrive at, even to leap to, the more meaningful conclusions which her work put forward. In the Rolle manuscripts the degree of judgment involved is particularly well hidden, obscured by the criteria Hope developed and by a human tendency to trust any good twentieth-century scholar as an authority. In her work on Rolle, Hope's method was at its best: she was careful in her application, her sample was as nearly complete as possible, and experience was a useful guide. But the *Ancrene Riwle* posed a different problem, one not so much of authorship as of reception and of practice. No one knew better than she the problems these questions presented.

The point is not that Hope's judgments, like all human opinions, were open to question. The point is that they were judgments, with considerable force, imagination, and insight behind them, a fact which the very orderly appearance of her work in print does something to obscure. There is a tendency to credit literary, historical, philosophical and theological criticism with imagination, but not the more severe judgments which attach to matters of canon, reception, and authorship. It is no favor, in these matters, to designate a work as imaginative, or even as particularly thoughtful. Facts are facts. But Hope's judgments rested on an ability to sympathize with persons who had died five hundred years earlier. After her death Joan Wake found this note in one of Hope's books: "It has been my good fortune to have spent forty years in research in medieval literary history, all to some degree concerning the characters and circumstances of individuals who once lived." This was the perspective from which her scholarship proceeded and from which she made her most important and imaginative discoveries.

In her early studies of the *Prick of Conscience* and the *Ancrene Riwle* Hope became acquainted with two late-fourteenth-century manuscripts, one in the Bodleian Library, Oxford, the other in the British Museum, which held her interest throughout her working life. These were the Vernon and the Simeon manuscripts, respectively, two of the most important collections of Middle English verse that have come down to us. They are also two of the largest. The Vernon manuscript, named after Colonel Edward Vernon, who gave the huge volume to the Bodleian Library, Oxford, in 1677, but whose family had owned it since the sixteenth century, now contains 341 of the original 420 vellum leaves, with about 80 lines to a column, and has a written area of about 23 by 16 inches. It weighs forty-eight pounds, and when it is studied in the Bodleian Library, it must be supported by a bookrest built especially for it.

The Simeon manuscript, named for Sir John Simeon (1815-70) who may simply have bought it, is much the same size, but less nearly complete. It contains 172 leaves of at least 380, and its format is different (for example, it is ruled for 85 to 90 lines to a column). Some of its text may have been influenced by the Vernon manuscript. The most important thing about both manuscripts is that they are written in English. At a time when the writing of manuscripts was slow and expensive (one scholar has estimated that the writing of Vernon alone probably took several years, and cost between 50 and 100 pounds, a staggering sum in the fifteenth century) the effort that went into producing such books was usually reserved for important Latin works, or, if in English, for works associated with the court or the nobility. Vernon and Simeon, on the contrary, contain a range of English religious texts in verse and in prose. Still, important differences there are. Some of the Vernon texts, such as the *Ancrene Riwle* and the A version of *Piers Plowman*, are not in Simeon, even when we have made allowance for missing folios. There are a few short items in Simeon which may not have been in Vernon. Yet the main focus of each manuscript is religious. Thus Vernon originally contained 137 separate items, including a portion of the South English Legendary, the Northern Homily Cycle, the *Prick of Conscience*, Richard Rolle's *Form of Perfect Living*, the *Stimulus amoris*, and the *Charter and Abbey of the Holy Ghost*, to mention only part of the contents. The main scribe of Vernon also worked on Simeon (one of four scribes), and there is every reason to believe that both manuscripts came from the same scriptorium, wherever that was.

Where that was interested Hope Allen. Even more, her concern to fix the circumstances of a manuscript's reception caused her to ask who read and who owned Vernon and Simeon, not merely who wrote them. Sometime in 1932 she made an important discovery in the Simeon manuscript. In the lower margin of folio 91 verso in that manuscript she detected the name "Joan Boun" faintly written. Subsequent investigation associated the name with Joan de Bohun, the wife of the tenth Earl of Hereford, Essex and Northampton, Humphrey de Bohun (d. 1372), and also the grandmother of King Henry V. Joan spent her last years at Walden Abbey, in Essex, where she died in 1419.

During one period of her studies, Hope treated the identification of Joan Bohun, and particularly the reading of the very indistinct inscription on the manuscript itself, with marked caution. In a piece she wrote about that time (it is undated, but appears to have been written in the early 1930s), she referred to the inscription as "scribbled" and as one "which seems to read 'Jon Boun.'" but by the late 1940s, writing to Ian Doyle, she spoke with confidence. Her concern with Joan Bohun was important in fixing the intellectual climate which produced not only the Vernon manuscript itself but also the astonishing variety of English religious texts which it contained. Unlike most of her contemporaries, a good deal is known about Joan Bohun before she entered the religious life. Her mother, Eleanor de Bohun, had been married to Thomas of Woodstock, Edward III's son and one of the more important lords appellant to King Richard II; Thomas has been treated in some detail by later scholars. King Edward himself arranged Eleanor's marriage to Thomas, his youngest surviving son, who was just eighteen when Eleanor's father, Humphrey de Bohun, the Earl of Hereford, died in 1373. Eleanor was one of the earl's two co-heirs, and the marriage had the advantage of providing for young Thomas (who later became Duke of Gloucester) without loss to the crown.

Anthony Goodman, writing in *The Loyal Conspiracy* (1971), suspects that Thomas may have been dissatisfied with the marriage, since the younger daughter, Mary, would inherit half of the de Bohun properties, and the earl's widow, Joan, was young enough long to enjoy her dower. During the mid-1370s, Thomas acquired several de Bohun properties, including, in October, 1376, Pleshy Castle, in Essex, famous for one of the finest lay libraries in England, containing eighty-three books. The books had been studied by M.V. Clarke in 1937, and seemed to show the interests of the de Bohun family, particularly Joan and Eleanor. Certain of the manuscripts have been identified; for example, National Library of Scotland manuscript 18.6.5 may be the complex devotional prayer book and psalter which Eleanor bequeathed to her daughter, also named Joan, and the library also seems to have been well supplied with books on chivalry and history, which were perhaps closer to Thomas' tastes. But the de Bohun family also enjoyed a familiar relationship with the Scrope family. Goodman points out that the two families had links through the Crusades, among them that Henry Scrope, Sir Stephen's father, had fought in Scotland with the Earl of Hereford's father and that both Sir Stephen and his brother Sir William were with the earl when Alexandria fell in 1365. The intellectual and religious associations between the two families depended on military and political ones but were none the worse for that. Thomas (as Duke of Gloucester) presented a breviary to Sir Henry Scrope, who was later involved in the plot against King Henry V and was executed in 1415; his arrest figures in Shakespeare's play. Sir Henry's will directed the celebration of masses for Gloucester and his wife, and he further bequeathed a manuscript containing, perhaps surprisingly, certain of Richard Rolle's works.

The Scropes, like the de Bohuns, had an interest not only in politics, which were rough even by fourteenth century standards (Gloucester was also involved in the conspiracy against Richard II), but in piety and devotion as well, and then as now these two concerns ran together easily. Piety seems not to have been limited to any one part of the family, for example, to the women, though there is more evidence for male interest in extremis, and certain of the more devotional manuscripts may be more closely identified with women in the families than with the men.

The Scropes had long interested Hope, who sometime in the mid-1920s had spotted the legacies which Geoffrey le Scrope, rector of Great Bowden, had left to anchorites of Hampole. Tentatively she identified the Scropes (and the FitzHughs, one of whose members, Henry FitzHugh, was the founder of Syon Abbey) as possibly being among Rolle's patrons, so establishing a link between some of the most powerful families in late-medieval England and some of the most important religious devotions.

These connections continued from the fourteenth to the sixteenth century, and in 1933, H. W. Lewer published, in the *Transactions* of the Essex Archaeological Society, the 1537 will of Lady Elizabeth Scrope, widow of the Earl of Oxford, which gives further evidence of the continuing devotional interests of the Scrope family. In 1958, Ian Doyle published, in the same place, a searching account of two of the countesses' manuscripts, British Library Harley manuscript 1706 and Bodleian Library manuscript Rawlinson liturgical f. 37, both rich in devotional associations. Doyle's study also establishes a connection between the Scrope family and Barking Abbey, one of the foremost English Benedictine nunneries, known for its founding in the seventh century foundation (it is mentioned in Bede; William the Conquerer established his court there immediately following his coronation) and for its later tradition of manuscript production and retention. Taken together all of these connec- tions and associations showed the extent to which the most powerful devotional texts, not excluding mystical ones, reached out beyond the oratory into the noblest households in the land. Not only do Vernon manuscript texts point to the interest of medieval women, whether nuns of Barking or the countess of Oxford, in devotion, but also they indicate that real concern for spiritual matters touched both genders and that the powerful, even when they turned to treason, looked to their souls with more than passing interest.

The study of medieval religious texts knows no bounds: mystical texts are close kin to devotional ones, and the aristocrat, the lord, even the traitor look naturally to the recluse and to the convent. Looking closely, Hope could see the most absolute medieval distinctions, between an- chorite and nobleman, between court and oratory, reach out and touch each other.

The de Bohun and Scrope families played an interesting if somewhat idiosyncratic part in the spiritual as well as the political life of their period, and the identification of their several contributions went beyond ques- tions of manuscript ownership to engage the most fundamental social and intellectual relationships of the period. But such insights were achieved only gradually, through examining ownership inscriptions and establish- ing identity. Hope had to attend to the more immediate problems associ- ated with such questions, though the larger matters appeared in the distance. Since the Simeon manuscript has a post-1382 date, it is possible that it too was associated with the abbey in which Joan de Bohun was enclosed, not necessarily as a place of production but perhaps as a place of retention.

Although Hope never published her work on the Vernon manuscript, having been diverted by her later discovery of the *Book of Margery Kempe*, she made up her mind about most of the problems she had identified and in later years was willing to reveal her findings to interested scholars. The clearest account of her thinking occurs in a letter of November 23, 1947 to Ian Doyle, then a graduate student at Cambridge, but with a dis- tinguished career before him. Writing from Sarasota Springs, Florida, where she had gone for her health, Hope worked without access to the considerable library she had amassed in Oneida. But whether it was the restorative air about her, the favorable impression she had formed of the very able young scholar whom she was addressing, the knowledge that her own return to Britain, or perhaps to health, was unlikely, or some combination of all of these factors, the fact was that she wrote with great candor, and at length, revealing not only what she thought but also much about her detailed, painstaking, occasionally erratic method of proceeding.

Her letter, remarkable if somewhat disconnected, cannot now be read as the last word on Vernon's origins, as can Doyle's penetrating introduction to the 1987 facsimile of Vernon, but the letter reveals much about her methods:

> I don't want to deprive you of any help my once-laborious researches on Vernon and Simeon could give you, and I remember the essentials – with time it has been advantageous that many complicated hypotheses have lost their cogency for me. The study of those two MSS is so difficult, thro their very bulk, that only the most clear-cut evidence is much worth considering, I now decide. What evidence points clearly to S. of Lichfield I hope to give you undogmatically. I agree that (as I think Miss Wood Leigh put it in the Cambridge Review) Manly-Rickert, or especially Manly, in his early work on Chaucer "narrowed the field" too much in identifications. This applies here. For example "Gruffith Smyth" [*a post-medieval owner's name written on the manuscript*] has written his name on Vernon in the 16th century. I think probably the man may be he of Venn's *Al. Cant.* (d. 1607) – associated with Northants, Colly Weston, etc. But the same name appears in Shrewsbury (the man d. 1554), and seems possibly Welsh. I have the wills of both men, and in a sense the duplication checks out both, for if records of two have survived, why may not records of more have been lost? Again, one could plaus[i]bly argue that the Simeons got the MS by any of nearly a half-dozen ways – Actually we can go beyond Awdri Norwood [*another later ownership inscription*]. And I conclude that we can't be sure that Sir John Simeon [*the owner who sold it to the British Museum*] did not buy it and *therefore* sell it to Museum (as he did, thro Torey). He made an address on MSS in which no word of it was given – his known (not interesting) MSS came from his Barrington ancestors. Somewhere some letter from him to one of his antiquarian correspond[e]nts – Thos Wright or so on – might give records of where he got it. And the positive identifica-

tion of the hand of those "early-modern" theological annotations might help. I tried to get a clue thro the parish registers at Bucklebury, Berks[hire] of his two generations of Simeon ancestors, rectors there (c. 1700)—but there was not so much writing there to compare with, as Mr. A.L. Humphryes remembered. Again, the Norwoods, of the family of Awdri I know, lived and were latterly recusants at Stanmore in Middlesex—a distinguished Oxford uncle—was it Dr. John Warner—yes, v. DNB—lived there—I looked at the registers and saw a rector's writing which looked similar but did not follow this up, though Mr. Percy Davenport told me he was an interesting person. After all, *here*, in the matter of the late prove-nance we have what (as I would not agree in all cases) could be called "a question of merely sentimental interest not affecting scholarship." For scholarship, what matters here is where the books were written.

I am glad you recognize that materials may be collected where the books were written—scribes, I also am sure, did not necessarily originate where they wrote. Such actual details as prove such circumstances should be emphasized, for the bearing on dialect studies.

But for Vernon and Simeon one thing that seems certain is that both came from the same scriptorium. The Vernon hand wrote part of Simeon, *both* MSS have the marginal reference to the book (a third volume evi-dently) to have been written by John Scryven for Dom Thos. Henley. I think the Vernon part of this annotation must have been done before binding. In any case the scriptorium for both MSS and *for the extra quire slightly later added to the beginning of Vernon* used *vinet* as a marginal note to illuminator, in a way not otherwise on record (it differs from that Sir Wm Craigie described on a Chaucer MS in N&Q [*Notes and Queries*]. In view of the weight of these volumes I think that they must have remained in the scriptorium during the addition of all this (some famous books were on hand 20 years). But as a conjecture more plaus[i]ble than any other I would suggest that Vernon represents the original collection, which was likely to have been made by someone specially interested in the recluse life, who revised the texts and copied over *a very long period*. The hand in V changes gradually. It seems to me—Miss D. M. B. Ellis pointed out to me a reference in a will of T[estamenta] E[boracensia] (I think Robert Wolvedon's) to a book written by an anchorite "Lichfield" I mean to write to York Registry for verification of a will for BMK, and shall ask also if this is the abbreviated place-name or a surname. I was struck by the fact that Scrope was bp [bishop] of Lichfield and wrote "on the scarcity of books" when Edmund Stafford was dean of York. The early use of Rolle and Hilton in V is notable—as well as Piers Pl[owman] (that might link with the

Simeon additions and Univ. 97)–of course a group knowing London is in question *v. infra*.... The Wm. Salt Soc. (the oldest register at Lich-field)...records Canon Thos Hanley (once in the rolls called Henley) as giving a "great" antiphoner, as also Canon Thos Haxey–at the right time. Hanley was incumbent of a living in Northants where the daughter of the squire (Alice Wakeland on whom a manor was settled 1408) became one of the anchoresses established under the influence of the Carmelite Thos Walden, whose surname was Netter–and whose birthplace–Walden–was in her last years the spiritual home of Joan Bohun (countess of Hereford, etc., mother of the countess of Stafford) whose name may be on the Simeon MS. Vernon begins in the added quire (added I think while still in the scriptorium), with the ME version of Aelred's Rule of Recluses done "by Thomas N."

A sign Vernon comes from a professional scriptorium is the fact that at one point a blank shield is included in the border. Nevertheless, the illuminator was subject to some sort of special influence of which the interpretation *might* tell us a good deal of scholarly import. Where the Spec. Vitae and the Prick come together (and Simeon by misplacing the couplet shows its derivative character which I believe existed in at least most of the book) two striking columbines are found in the border. Professor Rickert kindly pointed out to me that this flower was said to be of Lancastrian significance–she got that from *Bury Wills* where it is given without reference...

[*Later Hope plumbed the Stafford connections of Vernon, adding*]:

I now remember that the Scropes had an important estate in Staffs.–I think Thorpe Consta[n]tine (also Market Harborough in Northants). The York link of Edmund Stafford (later bp of Exeter) begins early–his mother was a Vernon. I got copied at Exeter a document as to a John Scryven associated with him there.

I have quoted less than half of this remarkable communication, which concludes with four long postscripts that reflect back on the problems raised, but this core speaks for itself. Not every point it raises has held up: for example, there is no evidence for a third manuscript on the model of Vernon and Simeon. But it is difficult, except in documents like this one, to catch the scholar at work. Even where the working notes, in Hope's case, her file cards and closely written notebooks, have survived, the questions they spoke to, the issues they engaged, escape unheard. Schol-arship, particularly as Hope practiced it, is indeed objective, but it does not come from a vacuum. For her, the importance of manuscripts was caught up in the questions that formed in her mind, so that matters of provenance were implicit in any attempt to establish significance. That significance reached back, in an almost direct line, to an ever-living past in which she found connections and associations that made intelligible the evidences of writing and of culture to which she gave her life. It was a very careful, very conscious choice.

In her work on Vernon and Simeon it is possible to catch glimpses in Hope's Oxford papers of the collaboration (not too strong a word) that she developed in the early 1930s with Dorothy Ellis, with whom she later became fast friends. It appears to have been Dorothy who was responsible for the discoveries (paid for by Hope at the rate of a guinea a day) of the details of Thomas Heneley's and John Scryvein's careers, through the Patent Rolls, Sir William Dugdale's *Monasticon Anglicanum*, and most of the appropriate genealogical and other books in Cambridge University Library. Ian Doyle's work on Vernon has now gone well beyond Hope's discoveries, but he has paid generous tribute to her pioneering efforts, undertaken at a time when there were few medievalists who shared her concerns.

Indeed it is useful to remember that, at the time Hope Allen was working, interest in manuscripts was for the most part confined to a critical examination of the texts they contained. Codicology, the study of manuscript books, was not far advanced, and was only rarely applied to English language manuscripts, particularly late medieval ones. Here as elsewhere, Hope Allen's work anticipated and to a degree precipitated later interest but remained different from what the discipline of codicology was to become. Her concern was rather for those who had read the manuscripts and for the requirements those readers might make of them.

One other reason for Hope's reluctance to publish the results of her work on Vernon and Simeon concerned the still-perplexing problem of priority. Did Simeon draw on Vernon, or do both rely on common sources? This question is not easily answered: certain lines present in Vernon are absent from Simeon, but the reverse is less frequently true. The best answer thus far (work is still continuing) appears to be that both manuscripts came from the same scriptorium, which had more than one copy available of certain of the works contained in the manuscripts. A Simeon scribe sometimes relied upon two or more manuscripts, and

Vernon was probably one of them. There is nothing astonishing about any of this, since it took a length of time for either manuscript to be written, and it may have seemed reasonable to consult whatever copies were at hand of whichever text was being written. But what is convenient and even sensible in the scriptorium is horribly difficult to puzzle out six hundred years later in a library. One text will seem to follow another closely, perhaps with a slip here or there, when suddenly it will include two lines not present in the supposed source manuscript, its exemplar. An understanding of the variety of ways in which scribes worked is a relatively recent advance in medieval studies, but for a scholar like Hope Allen, who placed so much emphasis on close and documented knowledge, such information was of utmost importance. The larger problems of author and audience remained, as they still do, and under the circumstances it is not difficult to understand why a meticulous scholar was reluctant to proceed, or to offer a solution where none had been established. Moreover, during the 1920s Hope was also engaged in what became her most important work, her study of Richard Rolle's manuscripts.

Just as her early studies on the *Prick of Conscience* led Hope to examine the Vernon manuscript, so they led her to what became her most important contribution to scholarship, her work on the fourteenth-century English mystic Richard Rolle. Thanks primarily to that work, it is possible to say with some confidence that Rolle was born about 1300, almost certainly at Thornton, near Pickering in Yorkshire, and studied at Oxford, where he seems to have been attached to the archbishop of Durham, Thomas Neville. He also may have studied for a time at the Sorbonne after leaving Oxford (apparently dissatisfied with the progress of his spiritual life there), though this is by no means certain, in spite of a fifteenth-century tradition that he did so. What is probable is that, at about the age of eighteen, he set off to become a hermit, initially on the estate of John Dalton, though subsequently (as he became better known) he took up residence in other places, finally settling near the convent of the Cistercian nuns at Hampole, in Yorkshire, where he died in 1349, probably of the plague.

Rolle's writings were numerous and were made more so in the fourteenth and fifteenth centuries by the medieval practice of attributing anonymous works to well-known authorities. Rolle's known works include commentaries on Scripture, especially on the Psalter (which he translated into English), the Book of Job and the Office for the Dead. He wrote English lyrics (which became influential) and books of devotion and spiritual direction in Latin and English, including the "Ego dormio," "The Commandment," and "The Form of Perfect Living." He also probably wrote a series of prose meditations in English. His Latin works include the prose tracts *Incendium amoris*, and *Emendatio vitae*, which were later translated into Middle English. Rolle was a learned man whose works on the Bible show the influence of the popular commentaries of Peter Lombard and Saint Augustine, and he appears to have been well acquainted too with Richard of Saint-Victor, Saint Bernard, and Saint Gregory.

From about 1910, and especially after 1920, Hope Allen examined as closely as she and her assistant and collaborator, J. A. Herbert, could, all the manuscripts containing works attributed to Richard Rolle. She employed four main criteria in identifying a work as Rolle's: dialect, attribution to Rolle in at least one manuscript, style, and theme. The last two criteria were especially difficult to apply: Rolle's style was imitated by countless followers, and his themes informed the spirituality of the next two centuries. There was thus, as in any other attribution, considerable room for dispute and for inference.

By the time Hope began what was to be her great study, she was no stranger to stylistic analysis. Her first important work, her article of 1910 in the Radcliffe College Monograph Series, *Studies in English and Comparative Literature*, no. 15, disputing Rolle's authorship of the *Prick of Conscience*, turned on stylistic grounds, attacking a fairly elaborate argument built up by the German scholar J. Ullmann (in *Englische Studien*, vol. 7) which identified Rolle's authorship largely on the grounds of stylistic peculiarities common both to the *Prick* and to the *Speculum vitae*. Hope attacked Ullmann's identification, but before 1910 she had no access to any text of the *Speculum*. It was not in any modern edition, and microfilm was unknown to early-twentieth-century scholarship; indeed it is difficult for modern scholars to imagine the problems serious students faced as recently as half a century ago.

One of the main purposes of Hope's visit to Europe in 1910 was to repair this omission. Thus in 1917 she published a paper in *PMLA* detailing her work, and , on the basis of her examination of thirty-one manuscripts of the *Speculum*, completely discredited Ullmann's conclusions. Her attack, written in war time of a German scholar, was as harsh as anything she subsequently put into print, and reported having

> discovered that the classifications of stylistic peculiarities which he [Ull-mann] applied to the two poems were for the most part derived—some-times *verbatim*—from three studies of the style of Old French writers....
> his use of the authors...amounts sometimes to plagiarism. Since the characteristics which he found that the two poems possessed in common are thus discovered not to be peculiar to them, no value of course remains in the use by Ullmann of these similarities as a criterion of common authorship (pp. 135–36).

In the same article she was concerned too with the relationship between the Latin *Speculum* and an English prose version of the same work which an earlier writer had suspected of having a Latin prose *Speculum* as a source. This scholar, who was French, Hope Allen treated with consideration, noting connections among an Anglo-Norman *Mirror*, the *Speculum*, its English version, and finally a later Middle English tract, not so much to ascertain authorship as to locate intellectual indebtedness. Still, the article stepped carefully around the problem of authorship and did not seek to prove more than it could.

The magnitude of Hope Allen's accomplishment in her remarkable five-hundred-page book on Richard Rolle (1927/28), is exemplified in two of the more complicated problems she encountered, one biographical, the other bibliographical. In the most important collection of medieval re-ligious tracts of its day, Carl Horstmann's *Yorkshire Writers*, a still-useful anthology which she probably read for the first time at Bryn Mawr, there appear three tracts attributed to Richard Rolle under the titles "Grace," "Prayer," and "Our Daily Work." Though none of the works were ascribed to Rolle in any manuscript, all of them bear some of the hallmarks Hope Allen sought in determining Rolle's authorship: their dialect was Northern; they showed a degree, even a high degree, of mystical awareness; and their style was not inappropriate. Horstmann, who was their first editor, had no doubts about their authenticity and insisted that they were "unquestionably" by Rolle. But Hope had doubts. For one thing, the fact that they were nowhere ascribed to Rolle was suspicious. For another, she doubted that the tracts were separate works. Her doubts increased when, in 1920, she was able to examine a manuscript

Horstmann had not seen, in which the works were clearly shown to be part of a larger work, a text known as *The Holy Book Gratia Dei*. The manuscript in question was sold at Sotheby's on October 21, 1920, as lot 137, to the London booksellers Maggs Brothers, who acquired it for the Huntington Library in California, where it remains, manuscript HM 148. Before dispatching it to California, Maggs Brothers very courteously permitted Hope to examine the manuscript, and it confirmed her doubts about Rolle's authorship.

A larger critical problem remained. *The Holy Book Gratia Dei* was made up of a large number of smaller tracts, all brought together and well organized, aimed at an audience which, whether clerical or lay, had to contend daily with the world and did not live in monastic isolation. But could not one of these adapted tracts have come from Rolle's pen? Here Hope hesitated, first deciding "no" and then "possibly." In her monograph she said "no" but did so on what have since seemed to scholars rather odd grounds. In the tract "Our Daily Work" she came upon an interesting passage in which the author, in a section on prayer and the contemplative life, speaks of the mystical comings and goings of the Divine Lover. It is one of the most clearly "mystical" sections of the work, and it is easy to see why it caught her attention. What is interesting, however, is that she rejected Rolle's authorship of the passage (and so of the tract in which it stood). She wrote in her book:

> As we have seen, Richard Rolle declared that mystical joy was perpetual, though most mystical writers felt it to be intermittent. The passage quoted shows, therefore, an essential divergence from his experience. It will also have shown the superior style of the piece, which would suggest that it was written by one of the leaders among fourteenth-century mystics. (p. 287)

But surely, scholars have since argued, that is no ground for rejection. The author may simply have meant that the experience of encounter did not go on forever, not that the pleasure of knowing God ended. Indeed, in 1929, the year after Hope's great monograph appeared, Geraldine Hodgson, the scholar whose work Hope had treated with scant regard in her monograph, produced a modernization of the work in question, *Rolle and "Our Daily Work,"* in which she attacked Hope's rejection and, as she believed, denigration of the work. She hammered the relatively simple point that I have just made, emphasizing, for example, that since Rolle says *dum* ("while") in the *Incendium amoris*, his own "ecstasy" must have come and gone. Throughout, Hodgson's tone stopped just short of being abusive, and it is hard to believe that she had not been affronted by Hope's attack on her rather sentimental biography of Rolle, and the tone of the exchange would not have induced Hope to recant. Subsequently, however, in her edition of Rolle's *English Writings* (1931), she described *The Holy Book Gratia Dei* as "a Northern compilation from various sources, one of which may have been lost English works of Rolle" (p. 57), and the remark seems slightly more accommodating than the comments she had published four years earlier:

> It is possible that scraps of lost works of his have been drawn on; the sections on *Grace*, *Prayer*, and *Daily Work*, suggest him more than the *Meditations*, though there is nothing in the latter that makes his authorship impossible. In spite of the reminiscences of his style in the section on *Daily Work*, however, the following would probably make his authorship impossible. (p. 286)

In fact, there was a larger issue at work which was unknown to either scholar. The text Horstmann had called *Daily Work* was part of another work, even before it was incorporated into *The Holy Book Gratia Dei*, a work which has since been identified. In Middle English it was called *A Ladder of Foure Ronges by the whiche Men Mowe Wele Clyme to Heuen*, a work which in its twelfth-century Latin source was ascribed often either to Saint Augustine or to Saint Bernard, but which was in fact the work of Guido II, prior of Grande-Chartreuse. Into this work three long passages had been interpolated. The first of these interpolations concerned the three degrees of grace, and was adopted from Hugo of Strasbourg's *Compendium theologicae veritatis*; it was this interpolated passage that found its way, via the Middle English *Ladder of Foure Ronges*, into *The Holy Book Gratia Dei*.

Thus subsequent study has borne out Hope Allen's rejection, but it may be worth noting that her intuitive grasp of the nature of late-medieval spirituality, and of Rolle's place therein, played an important if unscientific role in her identifications.

A second aspect of Hope Allen's monograph can be appreciated in this example of a biographical problem she encountered. In 1926 a French

Benedictine, Dom Maurice Noetinger, O.S.B., of Solesmes, took up the still-vexing problem of Rolle's studies at the Sorbonne and concluded that he had studied there, indeed, that he had been ordained there. Noetinger's reasons were not only the traditional ones, namely that there are certain manuscript references which connect Richard Rolle to the Sorbonne, and some late references to him in relevant documents, which have since been supplemented by others. He also pointed to one con- nected with the most important documentary source for Rolle's life: the *Office of St. Richard Hermit*, a work prepared, perhaps by or for the Cistercian nuns at Hampole, though this point is in dispute, in hopes of expediting Rolle's canonization.

The text contains certain related stories about Rolle's early life as an ascetic. Upon returning to Yorkshire from Oxford, Richard asked his sister to bring two of her gowns, one white and one gray, to him in the forest, intending to make of them a habit suitable for a hermit. She did so, evidently suspecting nothing. The young man then put on the white gown and placed the gray one over it, having first cut off the sleeves. His sister, alarmed by his actions, cried, "My brother is mad!" which caused Richard to threaten her and then to run away, lest he be brought back home against his will and prevented from taking up the hermit's life. Shortly thereafter, some miles away, he preached a sermon in a parish church which was heard by one John de Daulton (or Dalton), who may have known him already, and who, moved by the sermon, invited the young man to his home; there he sheltered him and became his protector.

These events took place, according to the *Office*, in Richard's nine- teenth year, that is, when he was eighteen years old, sometime around 1318. What sort of young man was he? As I have recounted the events, he seems, as he did to Hope Allen, unsophisticated and ardent, intent and uncompromising in his desire to follow the life of an ascetic in spite of all obstacles. He left Oxford, according to this account, to take up his vocation, which he followed throughout his life. But the available evi- dence will admit another interpretation: if we assume that Richard left Oxford not for Yorkshire but for Paris, there to continue his studies and become a priest, it is possible to conceive of him as a markedly more learned ascetic. The only certain date connected with Rolle, after all, is the date of his death, 1349. Hope Allen assumed that he was born about the turn of the century, but the date of his birth is uncertain, and it is possible that the account in the *Office* is inaccurate. If his study at Oxford was followed by further study, and perhaps ordination, in Paris, then the account in the *Office* of Rolle's sermon before John de Daulton which led to John's support of his subsequent austerities becomes easier to under' stand: as a university-educated cleric recently returned from Paris, he would have had access to the pulpit, particularly if he had been ordained. That his was no untutored mind most of his writings make clear, though the depth of his reading is still a matter of debate.

Thus the seemingly innocuous question whether Rolle studied at the Sorbonne has important implications. It affects our view of his character and the way we understand his work, factors that made it so important for Hope Allen. Noetinger, the chief proponent for the theory that there was a period in Paris, was one of Hope's correspondents. Focusing on the sermon which Rolle is reported to have preached to John de Daulton, he wrote in a British journal, *The Month* for 1926:

> If this Richard Rolle was really a Doctor, or at least a member of the Sorbonne, his life becomes much more easy to explain. When eighteen he leaves Oxford, but only to go to Paris and continue his studies there. Perhaps he was there in 1318, the date of the translation of the Blessed Magloir's shrine, to whom he alludes in "The Fire of Love" (ch. 13). As a student in Paris his life is such that he has reason to regret it afterwards; moreover, he begins to take pride in his scholastic success, and courts the titles and honours of the Church. But towards 1326 – perhaps under the influence of his ordination to the priesthood – grace becomes stronger. Tired of the world and of the scholastic disputes, he decides to become a hermit. He goes back home for a short while, adopts his odd costume, leaves his father. (pp. 28–9)

Thus when he decides to deliver a sermon at mass, there is nothing out of the ordinary in his decision; he is a Sorbonne student, after all.

Again Hope Allen was unconvinced. She thought a sojourn at the Sorbonne possible but unlikely, and she was unwilling to allow it any formative role in Richard Rolle's development. She was clearly reluctant to stand out against the collective judgment of Dom Noetinger and his monastery; she acknowledged particularly their expertise in finding pa' tristic allusions in Rolle, identifications which had implications for his training, but would never have urged a link with Paris on her own and regarded the suggestion with suspicion. Her Rolle, after all, was English to the bone, an ardent, even a somewhat Romantic, figure: he *might* have been to Paris, she could allow, but it didn't change him. He returned to Yorkshire, and there he found his vocation. Paris was a possible, but not a lasting influence.

Subsequent work by scholars has not been conclusive in this matter, though each one believes that he has said the last word. E. J. F. Arnould, a professor of French in Trinity College, Dublin, declared the matter settled in 1939 and republished his 1937 conclusions. According to him, the "myth" of Rolle's study in the Sorbonne was instigated by seventeenth-century French scholars who had misread their sources; in fact both Dom Noetinger and Hope Allen had depended on seventeenth-century transcriptions, thinking the originals were lost. But Arnould recovered the manuscripts in question and reported that their reference to Rolle was a misreading of "Richard Fitzralph." This seemed to undermine much of the evidence upon which earlier scholars had relied, but it did not by itself resolve the issue. The internal evidence remained, and recently a French scholar, Nicole Marzac, pointed out that a Prague manuscript of the fifteenth century links Rolle to the Sorbonne, thereby establishing a late-medieval tradition for the identification. This turn of events would not have surprised Hope Allen greatly, who as early as 1920 had identified a similar reference in a manuscript from northern Italy. The issue, which must still be regarded as unresolved, is of some importance for Rolle scholars, but a hesitant acceptance, not unlike Hope Allen's, may be the best conclusion to date.

A related point provided another complication, for in her study of Rolle's life Hope had identified one of Rolle's followers, Margaret de Kirkeby, with one Margaret le Boteler, who Hope thought, from the place-names associated with each woman, were the same person. The linking of the two names gave Margaret a rather long life, but it helped account for Rolle's last years, and Hope was not greatly concerned at her longevity since she had seen the same thing happen in Oneida, and believed it to be a distinct possibility.

In 1931, Geraldine Hodgson reentered the lists. That year she published *Office Psalms, from Rolle's Psalter and S. Augustine's Enarrationes*, and, in championing Dom Noetinger's theory, she made an interesting point. For a work well known to be Rolle's, his *Psalter*, could indeed depend on Augustine, as well as on Peter Lombard, for its origin, and if that is true, Rolle might indeed have read Peter in Paris, rather than Oxford. Further, it is indeed easier to explain Rolle's access not only to preaching but also to literary traditions if we assume a greater degree of learning than an abbreviated Oxford career might suggest. But nothing is certain. One danger of modern scholarship is that a learned modern scholar may assume a greater breadth of reference than a text actually warrants, and comment accordingly.

Like many other great works, *The Writings of Richard Rolle, Hermit of Hampole, and Materials for His Biography* is not an easy book to read, or even to consult. Part of the difficulty comes from the author's divided focus, which sought both to treat Richard Rolle himself and all his writings and also to discuss the manuscripts which were known (or thought) to contain his works. Hope divided her book according to the works Rolle had written, moving from the best attested to the least, from Latin to English, and grouping the manuscripts according to the attestations of authorship and ownership inscription. In theory that must have seemed an orderly and reasonable plan, but medieval manuscripts, and the problems they pose, are anything but orderly and reasonable. For one thing, Hope Allen sought to establish the authority of some manuscripts by reference to persons whom she and her scholar friends could identify. These identifications were searching, acute, and often convincing, but not always strictly relevant to the question of authorship. Occasionally too the organization of the volume fragmented some of the more interesting questions it sought to raise, such as the nature of Rolle's mysticism, the sources and effects of his language, and the physical experience, the heat, sweetness and song, of mysticism itself.

Yet the evidences of Richard Rolle did not fill all of Hope's hours during the 1920s. While she was working on her book, she found herself engaged in controversy, unwillingly, with McNabb over the *Ancrene Riwle*, and with Hodgson, though through it all she had support and consolation from her friend, J. A. Herbert. One other controversy which came up during this period particularly engaged her attention. For some time the topic of Oneida had retained interest for certain members of the British intelligentsia. When Pierrepont Noyes, president and general manager of the Oneida factories, had visited Britain in 1910, he had been dined by George Bernard Shaw and H. G. Wells. Wells had been an earlier visitor to Oneida and had written an account of the community in his book *The*

Future of America (1903). Shaw wrote in even more favorable terms in *Man and Superman*, published in the same year. At the dinner in 1910 Wells and Noyes renewed their friendship, and their interest in Oneida became better known in the community itself, which led to a series of events recounted in a letter from Hope to Shaw.

In 1924 a woman with strong connections to the original Oneida community arrived in London with the express purpose of explaining to George Bernard Shaw what the community had really been like. Hope became concerned that Oneida's reputation was in danger and undertook to write to Shaw on November 7, 1924. In her letter (copies of which are in Oxford and Syracuse) Hope insisted that the woman spoke from an "exceptional point of view," which concerned Hope because she thought that "what is said to a public man becomes in a sense official." She proceeded with this comment, one of the few statements about the community that she ever made in writing to an outsider:

> The Oneida Community, of which my parents and grandparents were members, seems to me the most intense and comprehensive experiment in human behavior ever made, and since it touched many persons very personally, selective estimates could be given that would offer striking contrasts. It so happens that Mrs. Smith, as perhaps she told you, is the only descendant of the old community who follows a manner of life related to that of the socialistic experiment of our ancestors. To the rest of us, the social novelties of the system seem to be an integral part of the theology, and to perish with that. Viewed as a mere experiment in human society without theological sanctions, I believed that the institution only served to illustrate the complications involved in any form of social organization. It bred as many problems and injustices as it solved or rectified. In any case, it could never be repeated without the condition of strong leadership, and a resultant strong organization of theological conviction and isolation from the world which gave it its pecular stability. Any one who borrowed license without its discipline would be violating the essential spirit of the institution.

But the end of this period of Hope's life came with a burst of energy. She finished her examination of Richard Rolle's manuscripts, and formulated her conclusions. She put aside her concern for Oneida. She turned at last not to thinking, but to getting her work into print. In doing so she returned to a former colleague.

Richard Rolle

In 1927 Carleton Brown was president of the Modern Language Association of America, and it was he who accepted her large manuscript for the MLA Monograph Series, thus putting into print a project begun under his direction some twenty years earlier. The printing by Oxford University Press was arranged for by Hope herself. The MLA had obtained a bid of $1,500 from a small American publisher for the printing when Hope wrote to Oxford, which Brown had already approached for an estimate, advising the press what the American publisher had offered. In response Oxford bid 367 pounds, 4 shillings, which, with the pound at $4.8725, amounted to $1,789.18. Hope then offered to buy seventy-seven copies at the full price of $7.50, so allowing the association (which made $3.75 on each copy sold) to make up the difference between the two bids. She did so for obvious reasons of prestige, but with a sense too that an English press would attend to such a work better than any other. The work appeared early in 1928 (partly because of a delay in passing proof; the book is dated 1927), and nothing quite like it had appeared before. Reviews were universally favorable, though Geraldine Hodgson was said to grumble to friends that Hope had stolen certain works away from Rolle, and in 1929 it was accorded the signal honor of receiving the Rose Mary Crashay Prize from the British Academy. The prize included a check for one hundred pounds, almost five hundred 1929 dollars. This award set the seal on what was a remarkable accomplishment. A notice appeared in the *New York Times*, and almost every scholar Hope had known, from Brown to Coulton, from Fr. Oliger to Dom Wilmart, sent congratulations.

It is possible to believe that Hope valued no congratulatons more highly than those she received from an old Oneida school friend, Carlotta Kinsley, who wrote to her November 21, 1929 in a letter now at Oxford:

> Your honor has created quite a furor here. First Chris first rang me up and fairly shouted over the phone, "Grovesnor read in the Times this morning that Hope has won a five hundred dollar prize" (shouting offside to Grovesnor to read her what it said—which she repeated to me). She explained that it was in an obscure corner of the paper, and I said after the delighted exclamation "How did he happen to see it?" She said "Oh, Grosvenor finds everything! I never saw anyone like him!" Can't you just hear her? A little while later Aunt Carrie Cragie (Whitten) called me up and asked for your address, "I suppose you saw the notice of her winning a

prize in the *Times* this morning?" Etc. she went on. Later I met Dorothy and she hailed me from across the street "Isn't it wonderful about Hope?" Etc. – Etc. – Grandma K[insley] came in to express her happiness over it and she said she had written to you. Now, my dear, keep your bonnet on and don't let your head get turned – 't wouldn't suit you at all.

Two earlier celebrations of the end of her work anticipated this one. On January 31, 1929, Hope sailed for Italy on a "grand tour" arranged for her niece Harriet Allen, just graduated from Mount Holyoke College. Landing first at Palermo, Sicily, they hired a car, Hope speaking Latin, not Italian, to the driver. Subsequently they travelled by car and train through Syracuse, Taormina, Naples, Rome, Florence, Como, Geneva and Paris. An accomplished amateur painter in later life, Harriet Allen attributes her first deep knowledge of painting to this extraordinary trip, made memorable also by several favors in respect to accommodation which Hope's academic connections afforded them. But she remembers too how Hope left her to herself in the museums while she herself turned to other occupations, primarily the reexamination of manuscripts she had studied two years earlier when she had toured France and Italy for one final cull of Rolle manuscripts before her great work went to press. Early in April the travelers arrived in Britain, Hope for a summer's work, Harriet to tour a country she still remembers vividly.

One other celebration occurred, probably in the summer of 1929, recorded by Joan Wake in 1966 on the back of a photograph (now in Oxford) of the small back garden at 116 Cheyne Walk:

> Back garden of 116 Cheyne Walk where the costermongers lived till M. Pallis bought them [Nos. 115 and 116] and turned them into a studio. In this yard, when Hope had finished her big R. Rolle & I a book of mine, we had a great bonfire of proofs, & danced and sang round it – Marietta, Hope, Mrs. Clark who jumped through the flames, the cook, Mrs. Mott, & Ernie the taxi driver her friend, & one or two others, costermongers, – a great party late into a summer night. The wind got up and the burning paper started to fly about – rather alarming.

The party was in one way an ending, but although she did not know it at the time, it was also a beginning. The stock market crash of 1929 was about to necessitate a new career, though only a part-time one. But it is to that new career, and to a new discovery, that I shall now turn.

5

MICHIGAN AND THE *BOOK OF MARGERY KEMPE*

h ope now began one of the most personally difficult periods of her life, when, following the 1929 Stock Market crash, she had to find paid employment. In 1931 she did so, with the Early Modern English Dictionary Project at the University of Michigan. It was while she was employed there that she made her single greatest manu-script discovery, in 1934, and it is to these two events, and their repercussions, that I shall turn in this chapter.

Upon the completion of a major project, the most common, and most irritating, question a scholar has to face is, What are you doing now? For Hope the answer was not difficult: under Kenneth Sisam's direction, and with Herbert's assistance, she went to work on a small volume of Rolle's English writings, which Oxford issued at its own expense in 1931. Yet even while it was moving through the press under Herbert's sharp eye, she had returned to her early interest in the *Ancrene Riwle*, an interest which her work on Rolle had all but submerged but to which she now turned with enthusiasm. Her reasons were complex, founded on manu-scripts she had examined, articles she had produced, and ideas she had generated, but no doubt too on a continuing, perhaps growing, interest in feminism. A student of Carey Thomas might be expected to treat women's issues with more than passing interest, but in the past Hope's concern had been more practical than theoretical. She had, through her books on Rolle, established herself not only as a scholar of some distinc-tion but as the preeminent American woman in the field of medieval literature, a somewhat ironic position for one who thought of herself as a historian. She had proved herself capable in the most complex areas of study then practiced. She had acquired a small but close group of friends

and had gained the confidence and respect of every medievalist of conse-
quence. Yet in returning to the *Ancrene Riwle*, she was engaging feminism
in a more direct way than she ever had before. Earlier she had taken an
interest first in those for whom the text had been written, then by whom
and when. Now she took up the effect the work had had, the areas of the
country in which it had become known, the early owners of the manuscripts in which it was preserved, and the significance of the translations
into Latin and Anglo-Norman (now that it was understood that the work
had been composed in English). These concerns were scholarly but had
important cultural implications. In 1932, R. W. Chambers' *The Continuity of English Prose* identified the *Ancrene Riwle* as one of the main
connecting links between prose of the Old English, and prose of the
modern period. Chambers' work was first published as part of the introduction to Elsie Hitchcock's edition of *Nicholas Harpsfield's Life of Sir
Thomas More* (Early English Text Society volume 186, republished by the
society as a separate volume in 1957). Chambers' work drew extensively
on Hope's but may also have been influenced by Edmund Gosse's address
in 1922 to the English Association, the secondary schools and university
level professional organization of English teachers. His talk was entitled
"The Continuity of Literature," and had paid tribute to

> the advance made in the study of Middle English, a district of literature
> almost entirely unsurveyed when I was a young man, but one absolutely
> essential to a student desirous of observing the history of poetry and prose
> in its continuity. For my own part, I may confess that neither I nor any
> other young student zealous for knowledge had any notion fifty years ago
> that Middle English Literature presented a bulky mass of important and
> interesting material. The period from 1150 to 1250 was practically a blank
> to us, for the telescope with which we tried to survey the scenery had a
> defect in that particular direction.

The remark must have registered with Chambers, who had himself
addressed the association the year before, though Gosse's lecture was
hardly avant-garde even in 1922, the same year Joyce's *Ulysses* appeared
in Paris, and today seems painfully dated. Against certain modernist
tendencies, indeed against modernism itself, Gosse had set literary continuity as a balance and a corrective. Remarking that "a monk of the twelfth
century had no intellectual perspective," Gosse took continuity to be the
product of the Renaissance, but one which "this inveterate passion for

modern actions and current movements" had placed in danger. His lecture assumed, and sought to maintain, an already established canon which he believed to be under threat, and he seems not to have appreciated that any examination of the somewhat illusory canon he was concerned with could only result in changing it, enfranchising new texts to be sure, but perhaps creating an altogether new perspective on earlier and later periods. But this Chambers did understand, and he set to work accordingly.

Although the particulars of Chambers' study have since been chal- lenged both by those who doubt that there was any continuity between Old English and modern prose and by those who believe that what continuity there was had been transmitted through Latin, Chambers' acceptance of the cultural importance and religious effect of the *Ancrene Riwle* was convincing. For Hope, however, who reasonably believed that Chambers' work drew on her own, even that was only part of the issue. Just as important was what the *Ancrene Riwle* showed about the role, by which she largely meant the education, of women in the late Middle Ages. In an early plan of the work, proposed to the American Council of Learned Societies in 1933, she noted:

> Anglo-Saxon nuns had been famous for their learning, and "Good Queen Maud" [who Hope believed had been connected with the foundation of Kilburn Abbey] had been largely educated in a nunnery. Perhaps the anchoresses of the *Ancrene Riwle* owed their learning to the native tradi- tion of feminine education. However, there was a general feminist move- ment in the twelfth century; it is notable that almost all the famous women of medieval Europe were the contemporaries of the Kilburn sisters: Eloise, Marie de France, Anna Commena – not to mention the German proph- etess-saints of the same epoch. The feminist movement of this period would make an interesting chapter of my investigation.

In her proposal to the council quoted above, she continued to hold the opinion that the work was written early in the twelfth century and that it was associated with Kilburn, a view that by the early 1930s many had come to doubt. In time she distanced herself from her early hypothesis (which, however, she never formally recanted) and became more con- cerned with the history of women in the period. She began planning an edition of selections from works related to the *Ancrene Riwle*: French and

Latin versions, derivative texts, anything which could help to illuminate its tradition.

This new project was one to which she brought enormous learning. During the 1920s Hope had acquired the sort of learning which it is difficult to appreciate, let alone describe. This learning she would soon transfer from the *Ancrene Riwle* to the *Book of Margery Kempe*, using it in part to defend Margery from certain gender-related charges of hysteria, in part to establish what she believed to be the mystical quality of Margery's spirituality.

During this period too her range of associations widened. When she paid a visit to Oxford, C. T. Onions invited her to Sunday lunch, and years later she left an impression of the occasion in a rambling letter to Mabel Day, dated March 16, 1949. She recalled that her host

> had a splendid study full of books and I got always from him the splendid sense of work done *con amore*. But the entrance hall was marked by the antics of I don't know how many dogs—there were also various Persian cats, I don't know how many rabbits and love-birds—I think three allot-ments were reported. Mrs. Onions (who was said to have been a pretty pupil of his) was still good-looking, silent—evidently most active in every possible way to support her ten children (but the eldest boy was in New Zealand from boyhood). She bred all these animals for prizes and profit, and must have been a most remarkable woman. There were about 7 children at the board, and it would have taken a dentist a year at least to give necessary repairs to their teeth.

Not long after the publication of her edition of Rolle's English writings, at the age of fifty, Hope made her last close English friend, Dorothy M. B. Ellis. She had known Dorothy since the mid-1920s, when she heard from a correspondent (probably Margaret Deanesly) about a lecture a Miss Ellis had given on Rolle, in which she had mentioned having found the source, in Ælred's *De vita eremitica*, of the *Regula heremitorum*, a work long attributed to Rolle. Hope wrote identifying herself and making inquiries. Correspondence (most of which is now preserved in the Bodleian Library) followed, and personal attachment quickly supplanted the academic one. Dorothy Ellis, it transpired, was a student of English hermits whose work had been anticipated by the publication in 1914 of Rotha Mary Clay's book on the subject, and who was now working on the Cambridgeshire volume of the Victorian County History, describing ecclesiastical architecture. Her contribution, completed by 1939, appeared in 1948. One of the first women to graduate from Cambridge (her college was Newnham), in French and then in English medieval studies, she was financially self-sufficient, and followed, as Hope did, the life of an independent scholar, addressing her work with the seriousness and attention it required. But she had too a lightness of touch that Hope lacked. In 1912 she had published *The Light-Bearers: A Missionary Pageant*, an outdoor allegorical pageant for children in which a character named England, after sending Saint Boniface and Saint Willibroad to the Continent at the behest of Saint George, falls asleep, only to be awakened by Faith, Love, and Hope, who call forth the nations (including America, represented by a native) under the banners of the Society for the Propagation of the Gospel and the Church Missionary Society. The production, saturated in medieval allusion, has a charm which even its naive imperialism does not quite obscure. England's final speech runs thus:

> God give to me the gift of justice, I
> Will justly rule, and seek his righteousness
> Where rule is given me. I bring to him
> The liberty he sends to the oppressed
> Through me and my good servants through the world.

In her intelligence, interests, and range of accomplishments, Dorothy Ellis represented a kind of traditional Toryism which has now been all but submerged. Her interests were education, housing and history. She belonged to various educational and learned societies, including the Northamptonshire Record Society (like Hope, she was a friend of Joan Wake) and the British Records Association, but she was also active in the Cambridgeshire Preservation Society, the Suffolk Preservation Society (for which she was a regional correspondent), and the Suffolk Institute of Archaeology. She had too a special interest in housing for the poor and worked with the Bethnal Green Housing Association, the Lambeth Housing Association, and the Cambridgeshire Cottage Improvement Society. She was on the local Poor Law committees, and on the Diocesan Board of Dilapidations. In all of these her twin loyalties to the Church of England and the Conservative party showed themselves to full advantage. Her interests in education were no less pronounced, and she was manager of All Saints School, and governor of the Newmarket Grammar

School. She was on the Diocesan Board of Education and taught in the Sunday School at Saint Mary's Church from 1923 to 1950. These larger commitments apart, she was a Girl Guides commissioner, a member of a committee for the Boy Scouts, and active in the Family Welfare Association, the Mental After Care Association, the Society for the Blind, and the Red Cross. During World War I she served as a volunteer in France, and she collected clothing for families of servicemen during World War II. Politically she was said to be "a keen Conservative," and in time she became president of the Wood Ditton Ward Conservative Association and the North Wood Ditton and Cheveley Conservative Association.

I have cited her interests and associations less to emphasize their number (she was not active in all at once, and during a busy life shifted her interests and responsibilities) than to show the range of concerns which engaged her. She was throughout her life profoundly English and deeply Conservative, though her brand of conservativism, which was compassionate, active, intent on reform and on support of those she undoubtedly would have called "the needy," is now rather out of fashion in England. It was no doubt those concerns, among others, that attracted Hope Allen.

Not long after the correspondence began, Dorothy Ellis allowed Hope to inspect, indeed to draw upon, her working notes, which were extensive, and went well beyond the narrow brief she had from the Victoria County History. A letter survives in which Hope expresses not only gratitude but surprised admiration: here was a woman whose scholarship, integrity, learning and disposition she recognized as being in many ways like her own. The two met soon after the correspondence began and got on well. Dorothy Ellis agreed to undertake some searches primarily for enclosed women, in connection with Hope's work on the *Ancrene Riwle* and accepted Hope's offer of a guinea a day for the work. Hope paid the amount from her American Council of Learned Societies grant, and some early requests for receipts from Dorothy seem designed as much to encourage correspondence as for any reason. Hope was attracted to her from the first, and, once begun, the friendship ran deep. In the late 1930s Hope added this postscript to a letter (now in Oxford) dated only February 21:

> You may be amused to hear that after your cable last night I had a nightmare – I thought you announced you were going to be married – I was

in a torment to ask if to a clergyman, but did not dare to ask questions—I feared that in that case you would spend all your time on Sunday school and parish work!!

The friendship took two years to mature. Dorothy Ellis lived in a house in Newmarket with an aged companion, Miss Mary Caroline Mackaig, (d. April 20, 1943 aet. 69) who attended to the details of the house, leaving Dorothy free to pursue her scholarship and other interests. Her scholarship Hope constantly encouraged, writing on November 14, 1932, for example, that she had recently met with Professor Maurice Powicke and that he "was most interested about your work, and thought the repertory {of anchoresses and anchorites] could be published if you prepared it. Perhaps the historical society, he said. His interest would be paramount, I know. He is a charming man, and interested in just these subjects." On January 25, 1934, Hope again urged her friend to academic pursuits, remarking that "I hope that your committees are not being too voracious of your time. I feel the more at liberty to push to claims of your research because I think I have Miss McKaig {sic] on my side." Finally, in 1935, they projected, in a letter published in the *London Times*, the never-realized publication of a repertory of anchorites and anchoresses, which they planned to edit together.

In the early 1930s Hope returned to America to work for the *Early Modern English Dictionary* at the University of Michigan, a task which Albert Baugh had both recommended and arranged, since, with the collapse of the stockmarket and the subsequent decline in the fortunes of the Oneida factory, she now had to find alternative sources of income. For the next six years, until her finances stabilized, helped by three grants from the American Council of Learned Societies, she made yearly trips to Britain to continue her studies on the *Ancrene Riwle*. Between 1932 and 1934 her friendship with Dorothy Ellis developed.

More than a year after the publication of *Writings Ascribed to Richard Rolle* the most effective challenge yet to her work on *Ancrene Riwle* appeared. J. R. R. Tolkien's article of 1929 in *Essays and Studies* pointed out that in most respects the language of the version of the *Ancrene Riwle* preserved in Corpus Christi College Cambridge manuscript 402 is identical with the language of *Hali Meidenhad* contained in Bodleian Library manuscript Bodley 34. Although subsequent work by a number of scholars has somewhat qualified the closeness of the identification Tolkien made, the article remains a landmark, indicating the importance of the Corpus Christi manuscript and the necessity of looking beyond the *Ancrene Riwle* itself to the larger circumstances of its composition.

In his examination Tolkien remarked that he found considerations of audience "sentimental," an unmistakable allusion to Hope Allen's work. He further added that the language which stood in the two manuscripts he had studied was unlikely to have been derived, or "translated," from an earlier version in a different dialect. Rather, he believed, that there were circumstances attached to the Corpus Christi version which indicated that it was closest to the original version, responsive to a particular school or to a single religious and linguistic authority. This last point caused a good deal of debate, and most scholars now believe that Tolkien some-what overstated his case, partly to anticipate the objection that there was a version earlier than the one preserved in the Corpus manuscript. By insisting on the superiority of Corpus he was effectively disproving Hope Allen's contention that the work was written in the early twelfth century and so could have been associated with Kilburn. His philological analysis showed that the work was more probably written in the late twelfth or early thirteenth century, and this contention has stood the test of time.

Tolkien's article appeared just in time for Hope Allen to add a reference to it at the end of her *PMLA* article "On the Author of the *Ancren Riwle*" (1929), which was in galley proofs, noting but dissenting from some of the conclusions and insisting, somewhat misleadingly, that they were tenta-tive. In fact, both the association with Kilburn and much of the "histor-ical" background Hope Allen had advanced were effectively undercut by Tolkien's study, which had the larger effect of shifting the mode of investigation from historical to philological grounds. Although subse-quent investigation continued, many of the questions Hope raised re-mained. Thus, for example, in 1966, E. J. Dobson insisted on a post-1215 date for the work and ten years later argued that it was composed at Wigmore Abbey, in Herefordshire, an Augustinian (and Victorine) foun-dation, for three anchoresses attached to Limebrook Priory, near Wig-more. His further conjecture that one Brian of Lingen, a secular canon of Wigmore, was the author and that Brian hid his name in a cryptogram has not been widely accepted. But Dobson was writing in the tradition that Hope Allen had established, though offering different answers. Important though the general direction of Tolkien's article undoubtedly was, it is possible to view his approach to the text as one which could be made to complement the approach, if not the answers, Hope Allen had advanced.

However affronted Hope may have been at the publication of Tolkien's article, she wrote to him shortly thereafter in a letter which is now lost, but to which, after an interval, he replied with great courtesy, and at length. There seems to have been no deepening of the acquaintance, though the intelligence and cordiality of Tolkien's tone were not lost on Hope. In a letter of July 2, 1934, to R. W. Chambers (now at Bryn Mawr), Hope describes his letter as

> one of the nicest most friendly and most interesting letters . . . about my work on A.R. that I ever had from anyone. It was exceedingly kind of him to write it, and I am very grateful. You were right that he did not mean anything personal against me in the apparently offensive sentences which he wrote. I am much relieved to get rid of the sense of disapproval which I had suffered from.

But Hope continued to pursue one point that she had raised with Tolkien elsewhere. She remained convinced that, since one scribe was responsible for writing the Vernon manuscript, it must be possible to speak of a dialect for the manuscript as a whole. By late August, 1933, having reawakened an old interest, she was in correspondence with Mary Serjeantson, associate editor of *The Year's Work in English Studies* and a member of the English faculty of Westfield College, of the University of London, who suggested on August 30 "South Shropshire or thereabouts. Would Lichfield diocese suit you?" Lichfield itself, she thought, "rather too far north." By February 5, 1934, she had worked through the index of Vernon (written by a different hand) and "could see no reason to suppose that it is not Lichfield." She published the index separately, but not until Hope's last return to America, when she resigned her academic post and entered an Anglican Benedictine community.

But if Hope was willing to leave to others philological study of Vernon (with its possible implications for her work on the *Ancrene Riwle*) she was far from abandoning her own work on the historical aspects of the work. Shortly before she transformed her program of work with her identification of the *Book of Margery Kempe*, she completed a short article on the

Ancrene Riwle, "The Three Daughters of Deorman," which appeared in the *PMLA* in 1935. The article shows Hope Allen at her best, moving confidently and with great erudition through a series of recondite texts, reconciling them almost effortlessly; and at her worst, for the conclusions toward which she was moving were becoming increasingly self-referential, increasingly distant from an engagement of the work.

Referring to her earlier studies of the origin and authorship of the work which had appeared in the same journal in 1918 and 1929, she proceeded to link the three enclosed anchoresses, Emma, Christina and Gunhilda, who she continued to believe were at Kilburn, with the "tres filie Deormanni" referred to in a royal writ, a suggestion she had first made in a letter published in the *Times Literary Supplement* of February 14, 1935, but whom she now linked to a royal writ of King Henry I. In making this new identification, Hope Allen was reaching back to a period she believed was years before the women were enclosed, and thus was forced to argue that "the extreme rarity of medieval trios of devout women" had made the identification inescapable.

Hope's scholarship was so wide-ranging that it is difficult to be certain how she first came to make the link with Henry. One possible source can be found in the work of a young London antiquarian, John James Park, who in 1814, at the age of nineteen, published *The Topography and Natural History of Hampstead*. The book included a thirty-page section on Kilburn and also linked the priory to Henry I, citing certain of the documents to which Hope would turn also. Park, who later abandoned antiquarian for legal studies, closed his preface by reminding his reader that these "literary blandishments which have beguiled my youthful days" were "those of a person who has not yet attained the age of legal capacity." He argued, however, that the Kilburn "damsels were three maids of honour to Matilda, the queen of Henry the First." In her development of the regal associations of the priory, Hope continued to assume that "the Kilburn ladies" were those for whom the *Ancrene Riwle* had been written, and she now urged a link with "good Queen Maud," which is improbable given the lapse of time between the queen's death (1118) and the date she proposed for the founding of Kilburn (1127–28), and because, as one critic pointed out, there is no provision for prayers for the queen's soul in the tradition of Kilburn.

But in the queen's last years at Westminister, Hope Allen argued, three "pious girls" might well have come under her influence, and that of Abbot Gilbert, and the three could subsequently have received "very special favors" from the abbot of Westminster (upon whom Kilburn depended), as a result of that earlier association, perhaps when an effort was being made to effect the queen's canonization. The larger question, "Who were the three daughters of Deorman?" involved what Hope called "a most interesting genealogical study." The same passage which identified the three women in the royal writ as having received a donation from Westminster also identified their brother as having been named Ordgar. He was so designated, Hope concluded, because he "was probably" the head of the family at the time of the donation. This Ordgar she then identified with a London land owner and so with the "English Cnihtengild of London," which "might indicate that their family was of important Anglo-Saxon stock." This "probably" meant that Ordgar and his three sisters were children of the Domesday Book's tenant-in-chief "Deorman of London." But *that* Ordgar died before 1130, when his brother, Tierri, son of Derman, "seems to be" in possession of his property; Tierri was dead by 1148.

Tierri stood high in London social circles, and Hope indicated (from a series of charters which Dorothy Ellis had pointed out to her) that his daughter married William Blemund, "who gave his name to Bloomsbury." This was important, Hope thought, because it showed that "this important Anglo-Saxon family, a century after the conquest, had intermarried with the leading family of the Norman baronage." Further, Tierri's wife was a *cognata* of Gilbert de Clare, earl of Pembroke; and had not the Countess of Clare once owned the Cleopatra manuscript of the *Ancrene Riwle*? Hope realized that there were problems with the identifications she was making. "The relationship between Ordgar and Tierri is not proved," she admitted, "nor the identity of the two Deormans," but she believed that the link with Tierri was important and that it was "worth while to push the investigation of his family history to the uttermost." In fact, what she already believed, and what she was reserving for future studies, was that such an investigation would lead to the family of William the Conquerer himself, from which, she hoped to show, the *Ancrene Riwle* took its origin. This identification rested on the problematic identifications presented in her 1935 article, and was influenced too by other concerns of her friends. It was probably about this time that she, Joan Wake, and Dorothy Ellis began referring to themselves as "the three daughters of Deorman." In the following year certain of the interests of the group were fueled by Edward VII's proposed marriage to Mrs. Simpson, and the abdication crisis which followed.

The affair of Mrs. Simpson and the abdication in 1936 brought forth from Miss Mackaig (by this time known to Hope, as to all her other friends, as "Skay") the following remarks in an undated latter now in Oxford. No doubt part of the intention was to assure Hope that no anti-Americanism lurked in her feelings toward Mrs. Simpson, but the letter shows too the values which she, Dorothy and Hope shared:

> She [Mrs. Simpson] is one of those completely useless people for whom I have nothing but contempt. She and her friends just spend their time amusing themselves. Dorothy has some cousins who are rich people, & who never do *a thing* except play squash & bathe, or "winter sport." They do nothing for their poorer neighbors, & nothing for their country.

That a king should break the "most solemn vows that any human being can take" for such a woman was, to her, unthinkable. "How I hope," she concluded, that the king "will follow the path of Duty which lies clearly before him." Hope's own interest in the abdication was not unlike her tenuous association with Bloomsbury: it gave her the pleasure of observation and conversation. But the association with Dorothy and Skay gave her something else, something even her enduring friendship with Joan Wake and Marietta Pallis did not supply: a connection with an England which was at once familiar and deeply moving, a world in which she could recognize herself.

In the meantime, Hope was experiencing the effects of the worldwide economic depression. On October 1, 1931, her brother had written to her (in a letter which is now among the family papers) that he had sent a hundred pound draft to her credit. "When this is done, it won't leave you a very large balance here. . . around $200 left. Pierre [Noyes, the general manager] was saying yesterday that he didn't look for an improvement before next year." On July 14, 1932, Grosvenor had written again: "For the first time the factory is down on real short time; they are only giving about two days a week, I think. As long as we can't make money we must keep our investiments down, so we are running the factory very conservatively."

It was against a background of financial uncertainty, then, that Hope accepted a position as assistant editor of the *Early Modern English Dictionary* being prepared at the University of Michigan. Her financial situation was difficult, but not extreme. Throughout the 1930s she was concerned, for the sake of the academic projects she supported, to insist that the effects of the Depression should not be overstated and that it should be understood to be temporary. She wrote at least one article to this effect. It was never published, but she continued in the untenable conviction that, after 1935, the depression was drawing to an end.

Hope's years at the University of Michigan were important in more ways than she could have imagined. For one thing, it was her only experience of regular employment in an academic institution. Although she had no students, university life was everywhere about her, and, somewhat to her surprise, she liked it. It was also a homecoming to the larger nation which was her own. In time, to be sure, her relationship with one colleague made life difficult for her, but the fact remains that the University of Michigan was the one academic institution to which Hope committed herself, and one for which she retained a degree of affection.

Her work on the dictionary was congenial. In the distribution of words for study, she was allotted those concerned with mysticism, and also certain obscure words. It was the second group of words, not the first, which most engaged her. She had earlier recorded an interest in what she called "the influence of superstition upon vocabulary," and although she dealt with many words over the years, some were more memorable than others. One of the more curious was *bogey*, which she sought to associate both with the devil (whence *bugger up*, and *bogey man*) and with the hard mucus that forms in the nose; Hope believed there was a connection. She ascertained that the word was in common parlance by inquiring of certain (somewhat amazed) Oneida friends what they called the hard . . . etc. She carefully recorded local variants—*bugger*, for example, and *booger*—and came to believe that the second term was local, and perhaps of Dutch derivation. In 1936 she undertook correspondence with two Dutch scholars to discover its etymology. Her final study of the word, "Bogus, Etc.," appeared in *American Notes & Queries* in 1941, and was one of her last scholarly productions.

Throughout the time she worked on the dictionary, she put into print, primarily in letters to the *Times Literary Supplement* (May 23, June 27,

August 1, 1935; April 4, 1942) and *Notes and Queries* (June 22 and 29 and July 6, 1935) a rich variety of ideas and questions, which had the additional effect of keeping the dictionary before the public and perhaps lifting it in her colleagues' esteem. During this period too she sent to the *Times Literary Supplement* a number of letters on the provenance of *Ancrene Riwle* manuscripts, and three of these letters (March 22, 1934, February 8 and October 24, 1936) repay study even today. In them she treated with great discrimination the ownership inscriptions appearing in the manuscripts. At the end of the second and most important letter she gave her address as the University of Michigan. At the end of the others she simply signed her now well-known name. Quite apart from the real contribution they made to the study of the courtly and noble families in which the *Ancrene Riwle* circulated, they had the advantage of clarifying her own scholarly significance in Ann Arbor.

As important to Hope as her Michigan publications was her new friendship with Margaret Ogden, an assistant on the dictionary project. At the time she went to Michigan, the great majority of Hope's American friendships went back to Bryn Mawr or to Oneida, and a friendship with an intelligent, personable woman like Margaret Ogden gave her a plea- sure during her years at Ann Arbor that no institution by itself could have afforded her. Mrs. Ogden was interested in the world Hope had left in London, and she had heard of some of Hope's friends there. Inevitably Margaret Ogden's interest was caught by some of the more familiar names: J. R. R. Tolkien, for example, whom Hope described as a "fine man," but one who could be somewhat "difficult," or the Bloomsbury Group (Lytton Strachey's sister had been principal at Newnham), and it is possible to believe that Hope did not understate her own associations in the course of their discussions. But the friendship created a link between her old life and her new.

The friendship deepened, in spite of a certain formality which re- mained. Mrs. Ogden and her husband called Hope "Miss Allen," even when she began to call them by their first name, and Hope maintained her position by courteously suggesting unpublished texts for Margaret Ogden to edit, a sign of confidence and friendship that she extended to very few. With Margaret she also discussed other interests: Oneida, American Indian artifacts, jewelry, and book collecting (in later years Mrs. Ogden received gifts from London street markets and from Oneida).

Hope appears to have spoken as freely to her as she did to any other friend, and years later, when Tolkien's *The Hobbit* appeared in London, Hope sent the Ogdens a copy.

But Hope's personality did not engage everyone she met. Some kept their distance; with others well-defined formality seemed the best course. Not long after she arrived she met and was impressed by Sanford B. Meech, a young Yale Ph.D. who was working as an assistant on the *Middle English Dictionary*. For a brief period in 1934, after Samuel Moore died, Meech had been acting editor of the *Middle English Dictionary*, but he was shortly thereafter replaced by Thomas A. Knott, a distinguished medievalist.

The transition to Knott took place at a crucial time, however, for just then Hope was casting about for a collaborator to help her with the editing of a great discovery she had made before leaving England, the unique manuscript of the *Book of Margery Kempe*. Meech, who had earlier asked her to help him find a text to edit, at once came to mind. He was an apparently self-confident man, with hopes for a university position. He had a reputation for hard work and for getting things done. Like Hope, he gave the impression that he did not suffer fools gladly. It would not have escaped Hope's attention that he wore, ostentatiously, in the judgment of some of his colleagues, a Phi Beta Kappa key. Not long after she identified the manuscript, she wrote to him from London suggesting the collaboration and offering to approach the Early English Text Society for the necessary approval. He accepted in a letter to her dated October 7, 1934 (now preserved, with his other letters to her among the Allen family papers in Oneida). Hope's offer was the single greatest misjudgment of her academic career.

At the time of her offer, and indeed at the time of the discovery of the *Book of Margery Kempe*, Hope was a recognized authority in Britain as well as in America, in the field of medieval English mystical and devotional manuscripts. In the summer of 1934 she was in London at a time in July when most British scholars are on vacation, and it was then that Colonel William Erdeswick Ignatius Butler-Bowdon, a Norfolk landowner, brought to the Victoria and Albert Museum, in South Kensington, a small, thick fifteenth-century manuscript which had been in his family for generations. In other circumstances he would probably have been directed to the British Museum, but Butler-Bowdon owned a number of medieval artifacts, some of which he had brought to the Victoria and Albert (or to the Museum of South Kensington, as it was better known) for identification (one of these, a fourteenth-century English liturgical vestment of great beauty and rarity, now known as the Butler-Bowdon cope, is preserved in the museum today). He was thus familiar to the staff, and they welcomed his latest inquiry. It was well for Hope that they did so. The authorities looked at the manuscript, judged (from Margery Kempe's proclaimed revelations) that it was a mystical manuscript, and turned to the authorities they knew: Dom Huddlesdon and M. R. James, both of whom were unavailable, and then Evelyn Underhill (whose book *Mysticism* is still read today). But she knew that her own knowledge in such matters was confined to the more familiar texts and pointed instead to her American cousin, Hope Allen, whose field it properly was. Hope went to the museum and made the identification in late July, 1934.

From that point events moved quickly: too quickly, Hope later came to believe. She saw at once what an important find she had made. Joan Wake later told how she and some other friends met that summer at Hope's apartments to discuss their work and exhibit their discoveries. Joan reported having found some documents showing that, in the 1830s, the railroad had failed to come to Northampton not for reasons of local resistance among the fox-hunting gentry and farmers, as had been thought, but for reasons of gradient. She spoke volubly about her find until Hope, having listened for a bit, interrupted with *her* news. Scholarly publication is important, but there is a certain pleasure about telling knowledgeable friends when one has made a real discovery that nothing can equal.

It is clear at once that a scholarly edition of the *Book of Margery Kempe* would have to be undertaken, and Hope believed that there would be room for a popular edition too. When she raised the point, Colonel Butler-Bowdon was at first uninterested and seemed content to leave the details to her. She at once approached the Early English Text Society through Robin Flower, who sat on the EETS council. Flower remains to this day one of the best-remembered manuscript experts of the British Museum. A lively and energetic Yorkshireman with a Northern Irish family background, he was well known both for his learning (he had read more widely in the Irish manuscripts at the British Museum than anybody else) and what can only be called his humanity. In his early years he had written poetry; his best-known book was *Hymenaea and Other Poems*, published in 1918. Georgian in sentiment, it includes the poems "Peregrini Pro Amore Dei," which portrays a scholar reading in "ancient books all day," yet never able to penetrate "the inner secret thing they had to say." But sympathetic perception was Flower's own trademark, as his two later books, *The Western Island, or The Great Blasket* (1944) and *The Irish Tradition* (1947), show clearly. His learning was evident to all who knew him, though some regretted that he did not publish more than he did. But these were generally those who did not share his perfectionism, or understand how deeply committed he was to many of the most important scholarly organizations of his day.

When Hope appealed to him for help in interesting the council in an edition of her new discovery, he referred her to A. W. Pollard, director of the EETS, and Hope also communicated with Mabel Day, secretary and assistant director of the society, with whom she was already in contact concerning a series of editions of the *Ancrene Riwle* which she had been urging the EETS to publish. But in her advocacy Hope encountered a problem, one that would complicate her later dealings with the council, for she had come to believe that Chambers, also a member of the council, was too intent on assigning British editors to edit the volumes which the society would issue, and passing over good American ones. Hope's own relationship with Chambers remained good, and he became one of her supporters during the troubles with the edition of the *Book of Margery Kempe* which followed. On July 2, 1934, the same month in which Hope identified the manuscript, she had the delicate task of writing to Chambers on the unrelated matter of the *Ancrene Riwle*, reminding him that the transcription of one particularly difficult and important Anglo-Norman manuscript of the *Ancrene Riwle* was being undertaken for her by her friend J. A. Herbert and paid for through her grant from the American Council of Learned Societies. She further felt herself called upon to suggest that American grant giving bodies would be unlikely to offer support "unless American editors are working from the beginning."

The next day she wrote again, having just heard from Sir William Craigie that there was to be a meeting of the EETS council on (ironically) July 4, which Craigie could not attend, but at which she thought the issue of American editors might come up, so she "ventured to write one or two things" that she, Flower and F. N. Robinson, of Harvard, had discussed in the summer of 1933, apparently at Hope's instigation, concerning certain "informal soundings" Robinson had taken from the American Council of Learned Societies concerning the degree of financial support for which ACLS might be approached. Initially these had not been promising because of the Depression, but Hope thought that some money would become available in time, provided "a definite scheme and time limit" were "laid down." The issue of "American cooperation" was relevant, Hope reported, and mentioned that Francis P. Magoun, of Harvard, and her old Bryn Mawr friend Charlotte D'Evelyn of Mount Holyoke College, were willing to participate. She noted too that she would be willing to permit Herbert's transcript to be used: "Of course since it was done for my research I do not think I ought to deliver it over for the edition till I can be sure that the work of putting it through the press will be soon." Twelve years later she added a penciled annotation to her copy of her letter of July 3 (now at Bryn Mawr) remarking that her letter to Chambers was "probably a landmark – instead of entering into my plans of international cooperation he seems to have rushed to get the most important MSS of AR assigned to English editors of his choosing, by EETS." Not all of Hope's relatively few later annotations can be trusted absolutely, but this one probably does reflect her thinking, whether mistaken or not, at the time.

Still, even if she was right, it was somewhat extraordinary for an independent American scholar to so influence a British institution (she noted later that some of the coolness she subsequently experienced from Pollard may have been due to her intervention). Hope was generally sensitive to the sort of anti-Americanism which is sometimes found among British academics – the belief that a republican neophyte will contaminate the pure waters of a higher culture – and she may have thought that Chambers harbored some such feeling, but such evidence as there is suggests that Chambers was simply concerned that American scholars not preempt the editions.

Hope was thus well known to the EETS council members when that body agreed to publish an edition of the *Book of Margery Kempe* and approved Sanford Meech as the editor of the text. To the director Hope had said that she had "lost interest" in the "linguistic" side, which she wished Meech to do, along with the text of the work itself. She would undertake to write a general introduction and notes on the work's mystical dimension, a field which, since her publications on Rolle, was indisputably her own. The council agreed, without any real inquiry into the terms of the collaboration, Pollard simply remarking that he hoped the scholarly edition might appear before the popular one.

But the popular edition soon presented problems. The owner of the manuscript, putting aside his earlier disinterest, decided to undertake the popular edition himself, since he estimated that the "general reader" at whom it was to aim might reasonably describe himself, who read "generally three or four books a week, of every description." He asked Hope to assist him by looking over his work, and Hope agreed, declining any payment. But the cooperation was intermittent at best. Hope found herself explaining why Margery being "vexed with spirits" could not be translated "pestered," and the colonel found himself hindered rather than helped by a scholar as meticulous as Hope, and one, moreover, whom he could not hurry. For her part Hope returned resolutely the colonel's generosity and candor, and, though concerned that his would be an "ultra-modern" edition, she remained convinced of his goodwill, and his ability to turn a phrase.

One aspect of Hope's work gave Colonel Butler-Bowdon pause, for Hope would frequently consult other scholars on details of points of interest, and the more he thought about this procedure, the less he liked it. He wanted his popular edition to appear quickly, before too much was known about the manuscript, so as to add to its impact. But he required a typed copy of his manuscript from which to work, and this Hope, through Sanford Meech, would supply.

Toward the end of fall, 1934, Hope shifted her interest from the popular to the scholarly edition. Her letter from London to Meech in Michigan offering the collaboration, was dated September 26, 1934, and on October 7 Meech wrote, as we have seen, (the letter is now in Oneida), to accept, assuring Hope that he would be honored to be associated with her in the edition. On November 2, Hope informed Meech that he had been accepted by the EETS, and on November 10, Meech replied deferentially, sending news of his dictionary and promising to work on the transcript of the manuscript, which he was making from rotographs over the winter, and to have it ready by June, 1935, when he expected to travel to Britain for further study. He also reported that he had written to Butler-Bowdon, agreeing not to publish any part of the manuscript or to write about it.

A subsequent letter dated December 13 shows how the task was proceeding. The actual task of transcription was undertaken by Meech's wife, Ruth, who typed directly from the rotographs; after dinner she and her husband would sit down and proofread her work. With Hope still in England (her long stays were possible because her position at the diction-ary was only part time) Meech read a paper which Hope had written announcing her discovery and describing the text at the Christmas meeting of the Modern Language Association in Philadelphia, adding some observations of his own. On December 27, 1934 Hope published a letter in the *London Times* announcing the discovery.

In the new year Hope returned to America and events took their course. Butler-Bowdon wrote to the publisher Faber and Faber about his edition, and a brief correspondence between Hope and T. S. Eliot followed, influenced by Hope's friendship with Hope Mirrlees, an Oxford friend whom Eliot also knew. Hope's reservations about Butler-Bowdon's accuracy emerge in a letter from her to Eliot dated June 24, 1935 (a copy is now at Bryn Mawr), which did the colonel no service. In any event, it was Jonathan Cape, not Faber, who published the popular edition.

Winter and spring, 1935, were relatively uneventful. Ruth Meech continued her transcription, a copy of which was sent to Butler-Bowdon. With the end of the academic year the Meeches prepared to go to England; Hope would follow toward the end of August. But before leaving, Meech sent a short letter to the *Times Literary Supplement*, which appeared on June 20, announcing his trip, requesting any informa-tion, and giving an address where he could be reached in London. In the letter he identified the work as Hope's discovery, mentioning her letter in the *Times* of the previous December, but not her part in the projected edition. The letter, which was reprinted in four local English newspapers, was the first public account of the EETS edition, and for all practical purposes it identified Meech alone as the editor. But these were early days yet, and the collaboration was still intact.

Yet Hope became aware that something was in the wind. That June Chambers was to take up an invitation to lecture in the Huntington Library in California on the subject of late-medieval English prose, and he wished to include Margery's *Book*. He applied to Hope for permission to do so and to obtain a copy, and she in turn addressed Butler-Bowdon, stressing the usefulness of Chambers' interest. He agreed but insisted on secrecy: Chambers was to show the text to no one. On June 26, 1935, Hope wired Chambers from Oneida to that effect, asking too that the rotographs be returned to her in London at the end of August. On July 10 she wrote at length, and it is clear that her suspicions had been aroused. She now reported what she called "a special embarrassment":

> I have found that when Mr. Meech was assigned the editing of the text it was assumed in some quarters that I had given up all collaboration, whereas I made clear to Dr. Flower at the time the assignments were made that I was to contribute the part that lay within the path of my research on Rolle. Mr. Meech understood perfectly, and I am sure everything will come out all right in the end, but at the present time I am occasionally put in the hateful situation of giving the reminder "I am writing the Introduction, and the notes on Mysticism". That fact has nothing to do with your work for the lectures, but I felt it important for you to understand the general arrangement.

Her belief that Meech "understood perfectly" was not shaken by a letter from Meech on June 25, in which he recorded his surprise that Butler-Bowdon had given permission for Chambers to see the rotographs but reasoned, as Hope had, that the publicity would help the American sales. He hoped Chambers would not anticipate anything she might wish to say in her introduction (a clear indication of the fact that he understood that her introduction was to be general) and concluded by assuring her of his cooperation and promising to mention her thirty-page introduction and her notes on mysticism to those he met.

Meech's next letter came a month later, dated July 28. By then he had met Colonel Butler-Bowdon and confessed himself entirely captivated. He had gotten on well, he believed, because of the accuracy of his transcripts, and he reported that Butler-Bowdon had urged him to be expansive with his linguistic introduction and historical notes.

Toward the end of August, 1935, Hope was in London, and on the fourteenth she was in touch with Mabel Day at EETS, arranging for an interview to discuss "some details about the general introduction, and the notes on mysticism, which were the part of your edition of Margery Kempe which I reserved when I suggested Mr. Meech for the rest of the work." She also raised the question of Herbert's transcription of the

Anglo-Norman text of the *Ancrene Riwle* and about the same time dispatched a postcard to the Meeches at King's Lynn, offering to go up to meet with them, but the card missed them, and the meeting never took place. Shortly thereafter she wrote again, raising the matter she had probably wanted to discuss: the omission of her name from the *TLS* letter of the previous June. On August 24, Meech replied briefly. He had not mentioned her because he wanted to send only a short letter and because he thought reference to her introduction unnecessary. He had, however, spoken of it to Mabel Day and Flower, the two people he thought were most involved. He also mentioned, as he had before, the names of local persons referred to in the *Book of Margery Kempe* whom he had located in the county records he had been examining.

Meanwhile, Hope's negotiations over Herbert's *Ancrene Riwle* tran-script continued in London. She was trying not to be difficult but to guard what she took to be the ACLS, and more broadly the American, interests in the project. She declined to turn the ACLS money over to the EETS, an alternative she had herself mooted earlier, because the grant had been directed to her; she was, however, willing to turn Herbert's transcript over to the "young editors" whom the society would designate but wanted to avoid the impression that Herbert was working under their "direct supervision." She also noted that Meech would sail for the United States on September 6, and would be in London a few days earlier. Could Day discuss with him the date of appearance of the edition? She would also meet with him herself before he left.

In a later description of the events surrounding the collaboration which Hope wrote for an adjudication of the matter in Michigan, she noted that another event of some importance had taken place that summer. Meech had written to Flower calling into question Hope's collaboration, she said, and insisting on certain claims. Hope had wanted Butler-Bowdon's manu-script kept at the British Museum for a final checking, but Meech had thought that unnecessary, and he wanted to be as helpful as possible to Butler-Bowdon, who had told him of Hope's request. Further checking was not required, Meech had insisted; the manuscript should be returned to its owner. Also, no changes were to be made in the text, which was, after all, his responsibility.

But Meech's choice of correspondent was not particularly astute. Hope and Flower were old friends, and it was to him she had turned to see whether EETS would accept the text: if anyone knew the conditions of collaboration, he did. When Meech's letter to Flower arrived at the British Museum, Hope happened to be working there, and was in fact in consultation with Dom Wilmart. Flower "burst in on me," she later recalled, "his eyes blazing." He declared that "Meech is cutting up rough" and thought the letter most unreasonable, particularly since the discovery, and much of the historical work, had been hers. In the end, though, Flower decided that Meech "was obviously a sensitive plant" and wrote a letter to conciliate, not to oppose, him. The storm passed.

Against this troubled and increasingly complicated backdrop, Hope and Meech met in London in early September, 1935. The meeting took place, Hope recalled, "with great difficulty," complicated by the fact that (as Hope believed) now Mrs. Meech "refused to speak with me or come to see me." Hope asked about many individual points: identifications, references to be checked, and the like, but found that her collaborator had confined himself to the collation of the manuscript, local record society publications, and the Lynn archives. They parted with the agreement that Hope would continue to investigate historical matters which Meech would later report; in effect, that she would supply him with information for his part of the historical background. Not long thereafter she and the Meeches met by chance, as scholars often do, on the porch of the British Museum. A somewhat improved climate had been achieved, and now "Mrs. Meech told me, as if a great favor, that they mentioned me as discovering the MS when they spoke of it."

Yet less than a week after the Meeches sailed, trouble began again. The first proof arrived from the printer on September 11, and Hope was horrified to discover that the work was now named *The Journal of Margery Kempe*. She wrote at once to Butler-Bowdon, whom she suspected of having made what was to her an amateurish mistake, and to Day, promising to send the colonel's reply and remarking that, as a result of the further research she had done and was doing, she now believed that she and Meech "should appear as joint editors."

Day wrote back at once, and with equal horror. The change of name had been her doing. She thought that a name should go in at once, and had suggested it. Meech had agreed. Hope wrote back on September 13, calming things. Day need not take the blame; Meech should have rejected the misnomer. All would be well. She mentioned in some detail the work left to do, what she had done and would do. She did not mention Meech's complaint to Flower, which clearly figured in her attitude.

She then wrote again to Butler-Bowdon, telling him that Day, not Meech, had been reponsible for the change. "I cannot feel that the blame is hers and I cannot understand why Mr. Meech did not inform me of the alteration (or experiment)," she wrote. But here she got a shock. On the next day the colonel replied. No change could be made in the title or in anything else, he insisted, without Meech's consent. He was the editor, and for anyone else (this clearly meant Hope) to make changes would prevent him from doing his work.

Later Hope noted that this reponse had made her so angry that she had broken off further scholarly communication, though a draft of an unsent letter shows her feelings at the time. It may have been Butler-Bowdon's letter which made her write again to Day, safeguarding her part in the edition. She wired Meech in America and consulted Flower, who advised against sending her collaborator further information. She consulted Day, in person and by letter and wire, both about the trouble with Meech, from whom she anticipated an irate letter once he received hers about the title, and, less opportunely, about the Anglo-Norman edition of the *Ancrene Riwle*: she would, she said, propose a scholar of her acquaintance if the early offer she had made to C. T. Onions, before having approached the EETS, fell through.

On September 23, Meech sent from America his expected reply. All his previous communications had been handwritten; this one was typed. In it he gave vent to the frustrations he had been feeling, and though he seemed to give way to the matter of the title, he charged that Hope had implied that he had not been careful, cooperative, or even honest. Her cables, he wrote, were without meaning to him; perhaps she would send letters to explain them. Both Flower and Butler-Bowdon had told him that the responsibility for the text was his, and his it would remain. Two days later, on Septermber 25, he wrote again, a brief, handwritten note. He had second thoughts about the title. The work was to be called *The Treatise of Margery Kempe*. He had already written to Butler-Bowdon and Day about the change.

At length his letters arrived in London. On October 4, Hope wrote to Day about the proposed title change: "Tho at the opening 'treatise' is found, 'book' recurs thro the introduction. The words were obviously synonymous in the mind of the priest who wrote this part." But she agreed that "in Margery's own preface 'treatise' occurs twice." Still, the work was already in bibliographies as the *Book of Margery Kempe*, and it seemed to her that "treatise" would sound "very dull and forbidding to the general historically-minded reader." On October 7 Day replied, having referred the matter to Pollard, who thought "treatise" gave much the wrong impression and favored "book" as did Day herself. She would write to Meech, Day said, and hope for his agreement. On the nineteenth Meech wrote again to Hope, preserving appearances. He had heard from Day, and quite agreed. "Book" would do nicely, if Butler-Bowdon agreed. Meech noted that he had just finished working though the colonel's modernization and had made very few changes. Finally, he thought that their separate areas of responsibility were now clear and that their difficulties were at an end.

It was not to be. On November 5, Hope wrote to Meech, arguing that to "separate out the mysticism is not at all easy, since Margery's life was founded on that." She would therefore bring certain names into her introduction in a general way, but they would need a biographical note, too, which Meech could write. It was not a proposition Meech was likely to find attractive, nor did he. On November 14 he replied that they must stick to what had been agreed: he was to edit the text and attend to the life records and to the linguistics; she was to treat the mysticism. Now, he suggested, Hope was trying to encroach upon the life records. Anyone mentioned in the text, whatever their significance, fell within his sphere, not hers.

Hope at once turned to Pollard and to her friends in the EETS. Meech's account was either inaccurate or mistaken, she insisted in a memorandum addressed to Meech, which she prepared on November 27. As far as editing went, they were both editors. She had so referred to them in her lecture to the MLA in December, 1934, and certain areas would have to be, in the nature of things, shared between them. It seemed to her that Meech had "almost forgotten" that linguistics was his primary concern. "Life records" was his term. It was true that she had intended to limit her notes to mysticism,

> But I made it clear from the first that my Introduction . . . was to give a
> general historical synthesis of Margery, so far as I had original material. In

other words, I was to sum up the contributions to literary and social history made by this text, as well as the mystical, as you were to sum up the linguistics.

"By letter, at the outset, I stipulated that I was to be free to repeat in my introduction (from your notes) any discoveries which you might make in archives (of course, with acknowledgment to you). Later, at Ann Arbor, I made clear that I intended to touch on points of literary history, in cases where I had original material. In any case I should not dream of presenting to the EETS a whole introduction on mysticism. Even thirty pages or so, if confined narrowly to 'mysticism' would be unsuitable in this place.

In the end she did not send the memorandum to Meech but left it with Day, who was by now an ally. She also wrote to Pollard, the director, to enlist his aid, but here she encountered a problem. Pollard recalled only that "mysticism" had been reserved for Hope. Meech had been appointed the editor. On November 28, a soon as she heard from Pollard, Hope wrote to Day. She confessed herself "much surprised, and, frankly, appalled." It seemed to her that the EETS was "letting me down very badly." Day replied at once. Chambers was anxious to get in touch; could she see him before she left England on December 5? Hope could, and she wrote with more details. There was no "original agreement" as such, so she could not show one to Pollard. She had written earlier to Flower about terms of the collaboration, but her copies of the correspondence were in America, as, most unfortunately was Flower himself, who had been appointed Lowell Lecturer at Harvard, Woodward Lecturer at Yale, and Moody Lecturer at Chicago, among other engagements. He was expected back soon, but no one knew exactly when. Yet Hope believed that if the matter was to stand as Professor Pollard's letter implied she would have no choice but to withdraw from the edition. On December 29 another letter arrived from Pollard. He thought it unfortunate that the agreement with Meech had been verbal and insisted that it was only "a friendly desire to help" which impelled him to suggest that from the point of view of the EETS, Meech was in a strong position. The EETS Council was to meet at the end of the academic term, but he was afraid that Flower would not be present.

By this time Hope had decided to see the matter through. She put off her sailing until December 31, and then, by a stroke of luck, Flower returned from America, refreshed from his travel, informed about the agreement, and willing to become active on Hope's behalf. He knew the details of the discovery and the collaboration better than anyone else on the council, and his employment in America had by no means diminished his standing in London. The tide, it appeared, had turned.

The council met and acted greatly to Hope's advantage. It supported her version of the collaboration, which it wrote into the minutes, to prevent future misunderstandings. More to the point, Flower wrote a long letter to Meech, explaining things. On December 31, Hope sailed for America in what could reasonably be described as triumph.

Or so it seemed. She was not due in Michigan until April 20, 1936, so she went first to Northampton, Massachusetts, to visit her friend Esther Lowenthal, a Smith College economist, and then to work in the Harvard libraries. While she was there, she received a letter from Meech, who had heard from Flower. He wrote with courtesy, and on February 10, Hope replied in a similar vein, offering some suggestions about the text, and inquiring when he might finish his work on the linguistics. On March 2, Meech wrote again, but this time, Hope thought, he seemed to imply that nothing had changed. She answered on the third: "In your letter of March 2 you imply that my introduction is to be limited to mysticism, tho the contrary was arranged in the original correspondence, and laid down in Dr. Flower's recent letter to you." She warned him against using too much overlapping material, and in the end there was little contradiction in their efforts, though at this point Meech was threatening to point up their disagreements. On March 19 Hope left Northampton to visit her family in Oneida. By the end of April she was again in Ann Arbor, ready for her last major confrontation with her collaborator.

It began innocently enough. Thinking to mend things, Hope proposed a series of conferences so that each would know what the other was doing. But the meetings did not go well, and Hope found her collaborator's attitude "supercilious and languid." Finally she put it up to him:

> A friend says I am a good judge of character, but that I have been mistaken in you. I was mistaken in not realizing how touchy you were. But I still think I was not mistaken fundamentally – that there is some mystery. You have given no sign that you have looked up the original correspondence. I suspect you think that the owner wanted you to do the whole thing, and somehow I have put it over on him and on the EETS.

That brought out, she said, his raw feeling. He became very angry and told her what he thought of her; the description was not favorable. Enough was enough. She broke off their meetings, and appealed to the editors of their two dictionaries, Charles C. Freis of the *Early Modern English Dictionary*, and Thomas A. Knott of the *Middle English Dictionary*. She submitted to them a long memorandum describing the events as she understood them, together with all of the relevant correspondence, which she had carefully preserved, copies of her letters and Meech's letters to her from the beginning. The result, Hope felt, justified her. Writing to Day on June 19, she said she believed that Meech would adhere to the present arrangements, since he would need his superior's support when he sought further employment, and Knott had spoken of preserving "the decorum of the edition." But both understood that the days of close collaboration were at an end and were willing for independent intermediaries to prevent their contributions from overlapping.

On July 4, Hope returned to Britain for a summer's work. Her troubles, though not over, had abated. But they had taken their toll. The following September she was forced, by an illness which owed more than a little to her troubled collaboration, to defer her planned return to America. The *Book of Margery Kempe* and much of the subsequent scholarship which has depended upon it, bear witness to the strain of her increasingly bitter relationship with Sanford Meech.

Few academic collaborations are without their moments of stress, but fewer still are quite as unpleasant as the one which finally produced the *Book of Margery Kempe*. In the end an even larger compromise was reached: the work would be issued in two volumes, the first containing the text, philological matters, and the notes of both editors (Hope's initialed), the second dealing exclusively with the material related to the *Book* that Hope wished to print. This shift was necessary not only because of the difficult relationship between the collaborators and not only because the amount of material Hope wished to print had expanded but also because Hope's attitude toward Margery's mysticism was changing; indeed, that subject became the major concern of the last two decades of her life.

The struggle between the collaborators left its mark on the published volume. The matter of the title, for example, is more important than it first seems. Neither Day's *Journal* nor Meech's *Treatise* will serve, the first because of anachronistic connotations, the second because the book is not a "treatise" in any proper accurate sense. It is important to note that it was Meech who insisted that a split between the two editors' work should be enforced. Concerned with territory as he was, that must have seemed to him a logical course. He was, after all, the younger scholar, not as independent as Hope was even in the difficult 1930s. His position on the *Middle English Dictionary* was not permanent, and he wanted a university career. Much of the actual work of preparing the manuscript was his, and that work was extensive. Finally, Hope was a woman. Nowhere explicitly referred to, this fact seems to me to have influenced Meech's behavior throughout; it is simply impossible to believe that he would have treated a senior male colleague as he treated her. Meech wanted credit not only for establishing the text but also for producing the work.

The act of separating the mystical from the social elements in the *Book of Margery Kempe* is no easy matter. In theory Hope was to seek out and define connections between Margery and the larger mystical context to which she made frequent reference. Meech's focus was to be on the social, not the religious, context, and though this distinction seemed reasonable, it was unlikely to explain adequately the text as a whole. To do so, Hope must expand the meaning she attached to the term "mysticism" and consider its relationship to the larger culture of which Margery was a part. Mysticism had heretofore meant mystics, but Hope, an agnostic, was unlikely to be confined by a rigorous interpretation of who was and who was not a mystic. Yet that was exactly what Meech was insisting upon. Duplication of effort was to be kept to a minimum, and their efforts were not to go in tandem, so Hope could not influence what Meech included. But her own interest included material on anchorites (some of whom Margery had met), well-known persons like Julian of Norwich, and a whole range of enthusiastic practices which were clearly a part of the *Book*. Many of these interests Meech was now claiming. The situation was impossible. It enforced a definition of mysticism which was simply too narrow for the *Book* and its protagonist, and allowed nothing for the free play of ecstatic religious attitudes which are central to the *Book*'s interpretation.

For Hope the suffering, which is not too strong a word, that the collaboration enforced had another side. In her redefinition of what she wanted to say about the text, she developed a new way of thinking about the relationship between the mystical, by which she came to understand the religious, and the social, by which she came to mean the secular, aspects of the text. This consideration engendered a new train of thought, as we shall see. But there can be no doubt that the interest she took in the feminist implications of mysticism, her belief that the mysticism of women revealed something profound and essential about the condition of being a woman, owed much not only to her work on the *Ancrene Riwle* but also to her troubled collaboration with Meech. The *Ancrene Riwle*, after all, though not a mystical document, touched on the conditions of women in a way no other medieval text did. Partly as a result, Hope's approach to mysticism, though detailed and specific, had been linked primarily to the work of Richard Rolle. But now in Margery she began to see that Rolle's mysticism and the *Ancrene Riwle*'s feminism could be related. Although many of Hope's colleagues were quick to see Margery as an obvious extension of her work on Rolle (after all, were they not both mystics?) the connection with the *Ancrene Riwle* was less clear. And this was the connection that she was determined to pursue in spite of Meech's objections.

Toward the end of 1939 she had completed most of what was required of her for the first volume and could turn her attention to volume two, which was to be hers alone. But the decade drew to an end dramatically, as it had begun.

The day England declared war on Germany, Hope was in North-ampton, visiting Joan Wake. They heard the news on the wireless together. Too much the realist to believe in the promise of a short war, Hope knew at once what she must do. An unwell woman of fifty-five could not be of much use to a nation at war. She would return to America and do what she could from there. As before, she planned to be among of the first to return when the hostilities ended.

Still, one could never be sure of the future. She sent most of her books back to Oneida, and sold her half interest in No. 116 Cheyne Walk to Marietta Pallis. On September 6, 1939, having written a farewell postcard to Dorothy Ellis and Skay, she sailed from Liverpool. The trip, on an American liner so crowded that the few men and boys aboard were assigned "clinging space" in lifeboat drills, took eleven days, because it had to turn back into the war zone to rescue some thirty-two passengers and crew members from a torpedoed ship. She had left England for the last time. She would not return. Her work on the *Book of Margery Kempe* had all but come to an end, but the development of its implications, as I shall show in the next chapter, was about to begin.

6

ONEIDA AGAIN

This chapter returns with Hope to the United States in 1939 and treats her years there until her death in 1960. During that period she worked to encourage several editions of the *Ancrene Riwle*, and at the same time developed her own interpretation of late-medieval feminism. She did not live to see that interpretation into print, but its main outlines are clear, as I shall show in this chapter.

The war awakened Hope's interest in the larger world of international politics. Aware of her own British ancestry ("Thank God every drop of my blood is English!" she wrote to Joan Wake) she kept up with events carefully, deriving her most cherished reports from Dorothy Ellis's household, most often from Skay, whose age and weak heart prohibited her from taking an active role in the war effort, and who, particularly in the early days, wrote frequently. Skay's letters (many of which are now in Oxford), move from a suspicion, early in the war, when things were going badly, that the war was a conspiracy, to a heady realization that England stood alone, to a settled and confident assurance as the reality of the war was borne home. Thus on June 4, 1940, referring to the surrender of King Leopold of Belgium to the overwhelming German forces, she wrote:

> I feel convinced that the whole thing was a plot cooked up by Hitler and Leopold, and that the crown of the whole Low Countries was the carrot dangled before the nose of the donkey, as his prize for help and complicity. I had been so puzzled by the rush of the Germans just at the point where they *did* rush in, & now it all seems clear. I think that the shades of the hundreds of thousands of men who lie on the hill around Etaples must have been watching over the B.E.F. [British Expeditionary Force], and helping them.

It has been the most beautiful spring I ever remember, it came *very* late, but it has been *so* lovely, & none of those awful May frosts that ravage the crops so terribly. The garden looks lovely. Just now there are masses of Iris, *huge* ones very tall, quite 3½ feet & shorter, but equally brilliant, every shade of blue, purple & violet & yellow, from cream to gorgeous red brown. . . . Dorothy is sending all her papers, & yours, to my sister in Devonshire, as she says, if we *did* have to go off in a hurry she could not possibly take them, so she is sending them away, and hopes to be able to go down now & then & do a little work.

On July 29, 1941, after the fall of France, Skay wrote:

I feel that fairly frequent news of us is only due to one who cares as you do, & whose love & friendship is so deeply prized by us both. Well, here we are. All on our onsis, & ready for the fray, & the calm matter-of-fact way in which everyone goes about his or her business would do your heart good. You know the old song "Ye Mariners of England" of which I have always been very fond. My father used to sing it to me when I was a baby. "The spirits of your fathers, shall start from every wave," and *they do*."

Receiving such letters, Hope found herself despising those of her countrymen who urged conciliation, suspecting their motives and impugning their dissent. Thus she believed that Charles Lindbergh, who was notorious for his naive support of the America First Committee (some of whose members had Nazi sympathies), was acting as he was because he "wants to be American and has always known he wasn't. They say he really hates his mother, that she treated his father badly." In the same letter, dated February 17, 1941 (now in Oxford), she proudly declared that "England has given a new meaning to history" and reported that her London home in Cheyne Walk "stands miraculously in the midst of destruction." Heroism in the familiar drew her highest admiration. "Dr. Day heroically corrected last proof [of the *Book of Margery Kempe*] in air raid periods, took proof to shelters," she reported to Dorothy Ellis on a postcard dated September 19, 1940 (now in Oxford), and on April 18, 1941, she summarized to Dorothy her feelings about what must have seemed to be one of the darkest moments for the Allies. "British, Greeks, and JugoSlavs are battling hell at the moment," she wrote. "They bring new hope to the human race whatever the outcome of these battles—at least some considerable groups of the world still feel that honor matters."

The following years were busy ones for Hope's British friends. Dorothy

132

Ellis plunged into a number of activities, from the Red Cross to the many Newmarket organizations to which she gave her time and attention. Joan Wake continued her efforts on behalf of local history and became involved in preserving local records, some of which were in danger of being declared wastepaper and dedicated to the war effort. At a meeting of the British Records Society on November 13, 1939, at the Inner Temple, in London, Joan spoke on "The Work of Local Societies During War," and argued that the societies should be prepared to accept and store collections which might otherwise be lost. She was also concerned about the drop in voluntary subscriptions which local societies like hers would experience with higher taxation, and she wished to move a resolution bringing the matter before a new parliamentary committee and urging on M.P.s the need for greater economy on their part, as well.

But not all of the bad news Hope had from Britain concerned the war directly. In a letter of June 11, 1941 to Ruth Dean she acknowledged news of Dom Wilmart's death: "I found it most shocking—the most final finis written to old wonderful days in the Museum that I have yet seen." In the same letter she remarked that she was going to defer a study which would involve Dominican use of the *Ancrene Riwle*, because "on that subject Father McNabb jumps on me, takes words out of my mouth, and misinterprets them to such a degree I have not felt up to the ordeal—the last few years I have been tired and not willing to cope with such tiresome mares' nests as he creates."

Nor were her interests confined to the war. When J. Pierpont Morgan died in 1943, she noted that the long *New York Times* obituary mentioned his deathbed reading of the *Book of Margery Kempe*. Hope's interest in Morgan (one of whose secretaries she knew) had professional roots. Quite apart from his own manuscript collection, which today remains the largest and one of the richest in America, in 1929 Morgan had made the British Museum a loan of thirty thousand guineas, interest-free for one year, to help it acquire the Luttrell Psalter. The Psalter was written shortly before 1340 and was thus contemporary with Richard Rolle and contains in its margins an extraordinary collection of grotesques, religious illuminations, and startlingly realistic drawings of country life.

Hope greeted with relief America's own entrance into the war though she became aware at once of the sacrifices it would require of those around her. When she heard from Joan Wake that Skay, at the age of sixty-nine, had died, she wrote to Dorothy Ellis on May 26, 1943, that Skay had had "a heart and a mind so full of rich human experience and detail of varied life that I find myself wishing that I could remember *verbatim* so many of her conversations. . . . How cruelly you will miss her I can imagine." Hope had lost another link to her past, and all around her the war left nothing unchanged.

The last two decades of Hope's life present a problem for her biographer, as they do for students of medieval literature. The publication of her last important article came in 1940, the year after she returned to the United States; she died in 1960. During those twenty years all of her diminishing energies were directed toward the second volume of the *Book of Margery Kempe*, which never appeared, and to a number of related projects. Tubercular from childhood, she had developed osteoarthritis, a disease that progressively sapped her strength and ability to work. Finally all locomotion became difficult and painful. In her last years she was attended by nurses and restricted to the Mansion House of her youth and to afternoon drives with her nurse through the countryside she had loved since childhood.

But the severe physical restrictions came only in the mid-1950s; earlier she had been fully occupied. Indeed, in spite of her physical incapacity these years were intellectually creative, the time in which she reflected upon and drew into a new synthesis the detailed historical and paleographical evidence on which she had spent her life.

Thus Hope's academic studies continued. Soon after she returned to the United States in 1939, she began work again, having by now formed a substantial library in Oneida. Studies she had begun before, on the popular devotion to the Holy Name, for example, which went back to the 1920s, and on the Julian formulation of the *Benedictus Domine*, from the early 1930s, were now organized for the projected second volume. The present rather chaotic state of Hope's manuscripts can create the impression that her work was more diverse and subject to more false starts and wanderings than it in fact was. Her difficulties were associated with integration, not fragmentation. She often saw relationships that escaped others and became concerned with sometimes tenuous connections, at the expense of bringing an article to a close.

For example, sometime in the early 1930s Hope had discerned a relationship between Margery and the London skinner Henry Lovelich, whose Middle English translations of *Merlin* and *The History of the Holy Grail* had been published by the Early English Text Society. In 1944, when her friend Mabel Day, the secretary of the society, requested information about the progress of volume 2, it was the Lovelich connection that Hope stressed, in one of the few detailed descriptions she gave of work in hand. Writing to Day on April 6 of that year, she remarked:

> Mr. Meech did valuable notes, but entirely ignored the rolls. I have had to go over them, for I feel that the "Lynn revolution" which is such a notable incident of municipal history (witness Mrs. Green's *Town Life in the 15th Century*) had to be sketched into the background. It coincides with M's "conversion" and her family bore a leading part. After her father died her brother inherited part at least of the property, as Mr. Meech discovered— at the height of this trouble I find in the rolls that a writ was out to arrest him, but he was released by mainprise of 3 Londoners and 1 Norfolk man— the first-named of the former was Henry Lovelich, skinner of London, of whom EETS has in print several dull volumes—and the Norfolk man was step-son of HL, who I find married a rich Lynn widow with houses, quay etc. opposite St. Margaret's. Lovelich is said to have written at request of Henry Barton—also a skinner and also linked to Lynn. M's father-in-law was a skinner (Mr. Meech found out) with large dealings with Danzig. I find a letter from Richard II sent to Luebeck in 1388, to protest his imprisonment there. Mr. Meech shows near relatives were members of the Corpus Christi Guild—the London skinners were a Corpus Christi Guild— I wonder if that movement was used to combat Lollardry? I have long felt M put forward her spasms as the effect of the Holy Spirit thro the Sacrament—a nun of Stanbrook wrote something of the same sort. I have also noted with interest her long sojourns in London.

Hope had become concerned about the limitations of the published histories of Lynn (which have only recently been rectified) and on July 30, 1944 wrote to Day: "I want to make it a prime effect of my book to encourage production of two things—a book of Norfolk wills and a proper history of Lynn." By 1946, however, she had broadened the scope of her study. On April 26 of that year she wrote to Day: "My general line on BMK II as you perhaps know is to present it as a moment of the counter reformation of the early 15th century in England." On June 12 she added that "the early 15th century counter reformation in England" was to be the main theme of her introduction, which was to be long and would precede the texts and excerpts that would carry the burden of her argument. But the items to be included were never quite decided, though many of them appear in the list she had drawn up a decade earlier to illustrate the influence of the *Ancrene Riwle*. To this list she added other items, a Bodley sermon, a selection from *The Orchard of Syon*, or Marie d'Oignies, as her thinking was engaged by the larger religious and mystical topics of the *Book of Margery Kempe*. But she never set aside the more exacting historical studies which she rightly believed would have added much to our knowledge of Margery and her social connections, and it is a great pity that she never completed her second volume. Still, for twenty years the EETS continued to list the volume as "forthcoming."

In 1940 she published the last of her many works on the *Ancrene Riwle*: "Wynkyn de Worde and a Second French Compilation from the *Ancrene Riwle*, with a Description of the First," which appeared in a festschrift for Carleton Brown. He had been her first medieval teacher, and had sup-ported her throughout her career, publishing her great work on Rolle and articles on the *Ancrene Riwle* and supporting her grant applications. The article was a major one and was linked to three earlier articles in which she traced the effect of the *Ancrene Riwle* in late-medieval culture. These studies, as distinct from those which treated origin and ownership, have great value for modern students of the text, and her article on de Worde is the best of them.

In it, she pointed out that the *Treatise of Love*, a late Middle English work printed by Caxton's successor, the English printer Wynkyn de Worde, contained a rendering of large parts of the *Ancrene Riwle* and that these borrowings had been translated from an Anglo-Norman version in Trinity College Cambridge manuscript 883, R.14.7. The now lost version of *Ancrene Riwle* upon which de Worde's text was based, she believed, had already been much expanded from its source, an even earlier version of the *Ancrene Riwle*. Parts of it had been shifted about; for example, the section on sin in book four of the *Ancrene Riwle* had been detached to make a fifth book, and the opening liturgical sections had been omitted to make the *Riwle* "of practical utility to any devout person preparing for confession."

This was in itself an interesting and useful discovery: it established more clearly than any of her earlier studies that the *Riwle* had an important place in late-medieval culture, that it had crossed and recrossed linguistic barriers, and that it was thus a work to be reckoned with in Anglo-Norman, as well as in English. The expanded version of the *Ancrene Riwle* on which the *Treatise of Love* was founded Hope linked to a Benedictine house and suggested that it may have been dedicated to reading in the refectory, a use "which I had not thought of before." She also adduced certain links of the *Riwle* with Franciscans, particularly those men and women who took up the life of the recluse and so required more specific direction than the Franciscan rule provided. In one of her rare humorous remarks, Hope referred to "the spiritual direction by English friars of contemplative women – which is something very different from the diversion of women of less advanced piety, with which friars are commonly associated." Her post-1930 interests in the English nobility were in evidence in this study, not only in the noble owners of the Anglo-Norman versions of the *Ancrene Riwle* but also in noble recluses like Lady Leicester (enclosed near Canterbury) and Lady Mortimer (enclosed near Oxford), whom Dorothy Ellis had brought to her attention.

The Trinity manuscript seemed to Hope to show both fraternal and monastic features which gave it a special interest, particularly since she had come to believe, following Dorothy Ellis, that when the Franciscans finally did establish convents for women, they must have been enclosed. "Through three hundred years," she wrote, "we have seen the *Riwle* used, in varying degrees, as a practical rule of life – being adapted in some ways to suit special circumstances of a person or a group, by friars among others." But the new French version did not establish the original language of the *Riwle*, which Hope was still inclined to believe might have been French. The tract itself, however, was written for a culture which used French and English interchangeably, and thus she considered the linguistic evidence less important than the historical, and remained attentive to further associations with the Anglo-Norman nobility, which the new Trinity manuscript confirmed. The Wynkyn de Worde version with which she had begun her study, however, remained something of a mystery. What was clearly needed was an edition of the text, the importance of which her study of the Trinity manuscript had now made clear.

During this period she also undertook to write articles on Margery Kempe and Julian of Norwich for the *Encyclopaedia Britannica*. In the articles, which were never published, Hope concentrated her attention on Julian in particular, and on the problems her chronology exposed. Hope had thought about these matters in the past, and she now set out to do for Julian what she had done earlier and at much greater length, for Richard Rolle. Almost at once she ran into problems. Julian had not had Richard's fame, nor had she been advanced for canonization. As a result, subsequent references to her are rare, and must be excavated by scholars working diligently through county archives and local wills. Hope had done more than her share of such work, as certain scholarly manuscripts show, including a short memorandum Helen Gardner wrote in July, 1939, of a "Conversation with Miss Allen" (now in Oxford, in the possession of Dr. Anne Hudson): "Julian of Norwich. Julian anchoress at Carrow [in the Norwich suburbs] has extraordinary amount of legacies, every year, sometimes twice a year for c. 1426–1470 odd. Only one legacy to Julian of Norwich 1416. Gap of ten years before Carrow legacies suggests two separate women. Powerful families supported Carrow anchoress. . . . Was Julian [of Norwich] a virgin?" The last question may have been suggested to Hope by the reference to Julian as "Dame" in documents in the Norfolk Record Office, and shows her willingness to press beyond appearances. But the matter of her chronology engaged her attention deeply on her return to Oneida.

Hope was familiar with early printed sources relevant to Julian of Norwich, including Francis Bloomfield's early nineteenth-century *Essay Towards a Topographical History of the County of Norfolk*, a modest title for an eleven-volume work. For Julian (vol. IV, pp. 81–4), Bloomfield had had access to a manuscript owned by one Francis Peck, which is almost certainly the manuscript now in the British Library, Additional manuscript 37790. In describing the manuscript, Bloomfield had misdated it, writing 1443 instead of 1413, so adding thirty years to Julian's already long life. Like most other scholars, Hope had no difficulty seeing Bloomfield's error, but she hesitated to reject absolutely the later date, Bloomfield having written 1442 in another place, and thus made more difficulties for herself than she need have. In what she thought might be an appendix to her volume on Margery Kempe, she intended to float the possibility that Julian had lived longer, had indeed been a centenarian. But she was not certain that Margery had met Julian the Mystic, and not her successor in the anchorhold, Julian Lampit.

In her last years, removed from major libraries and association with fellow scholars, paradoxically she became less flexible in some of her judgments at the same time that her thought was becoming freer and more associative than it had for some time. But she was still much concerned with detail and could point out, for example, the difficulties of finding two recluses in the same place both named Julian. The pages she wrote on this particular aspect of Julian of Norwich show something of the range of reference she could command, as well as the confusion into which she, like all scholars, could be drawn. Reluctant simply to reject Bloomfield's dating, she was able to adduce associations which showed the complexity of the problem but which in the end shed little light. Still, her suggestion that certain of the references usually taken as referring to Julian of Norwich refer instead to another woman is commendably careful, and she was probably right too in finally insisting that Julian died not long after 1416.

During this period she developed a correspondence with Sister Anna Maria Reynolds, C.P., who had begun preparing an edition of Julian and who was the student of the British scholar R. M. Wilson, whom Hope knew slightly. Hope offered advice and encouragement, though she never came to know Sister Reynolds well and so was disinclined to advance her case with the EETS Council, where concern was expressed by those who thought themselves familiar with the difficulties under which members of religious orders often undertook scholarship, though Sister Reynolds believed that she faced a degree of anti-Catholicism as well. In the event, and after some hesitation, Hope offered what assistance she could, but Sister Reynolds did not complete the project. The work she did do, however, was acknowledged by James Walsh, S.J., and Edmund Colledge, O.S.A., in their introduction to the Toronto edition of Julian of Norwich, published in 1978.

During this period honors came her way. Charlotte D'Evelyn proposed her for a fellowship in the Medieval Academy of America, and after a time she was elected. The Academy was something of a closed shop and not notably well disposed toward women. On June 20, 1948, Hope wrote a letter to Dorothy Ellis (now in Oxford) expressing one of her few direct protests against the sexism she had experienced:

> I had a great honor—went to NY to the Annual Meeting of the Medieval Academy of America, held this year at the Morgan Library, to be inducted

as a fellow – the peculiar distinction rests on an injustice – there are 4 men and 3 women – one of these the Morgan Librarian, one a brilliant Arme-nian woman who is a pathfinder in Byzantine culture – I got in through a fluke because in her last years I saw much of Professor Nellie Nelson the historian who for years was the only woman – she told me she put me up but in the first year I was not taken – the Armenian was – then after N[ellie]'s death I was. They ought and will have more women eventually, I hope.

Her last important honor came from Bryn Mawr shortly before her death, when on June 4, 1960, at the time of the college's seventy-fifth anniversary convocation, she was designated one of its seventy-six most distinguished graduates. Ill health alone prevented her from traveling to receive the award, the announcement of which cheered her last months.

Hope's other scholarly activity in her later years concerned Oneida. In 1948, the centennial of its founding, she took an active part in the celebrations, assisted by Jane Rich, an admired younger friend in the community, with whom she discussed life in England as they arranged the exhibitions and worked on the community publication. During this period she also recorded memoirs and recollections of the older members, and her work was detailed and precise. Her efforts for the centennial, were extensive and time-consuming. She was concerned to preserve and iden-tify early photographs, and whatever artifacts she could identify from the first settlement, including the distinctive women's dress, with short skirts and pantaloons. The History Room in the Mansion House owes much to Hope's and Jane Rich's efforts.

Nor was her interest in Oneida history limited to the early settlement. She had long been interested in the Oneida Indians, and became active in recording their legends during her 1913 recovery. On December 19, 1925, she had taken down a number of Oneida tales from Anna Johnson, the wife of Josiah Johnson, one of the principal storytellers of the Oneida tribe. Hope wrote in a collection of ethnographic notes composed during the 1950s (now at Syracuse):

> I first knew Anna in 1912, when she was married to Si and living in Baptist's [a tribal member's] house, one of the (then) light and small Indian homesteads on the hill. Relations were close between the two Oneida [Indian] groups, who comprise families given at their request freehold, tax-free homes on the one-time reservation. In my childhood the Indians among

140

us in part still earned their living by sellng native wears for which they travelled considerable distances to get the materials in swamps, etc.

Hope was "inclined to think that in Si Johnson's life his power as a story-teller was his notable accomplishment. But almost certainly none of the white men with whom he worked peacefully in farms or factories would have suspected this. He was extremely shy, and also delicate."

In Si Johnson, Hope saw something of the artist who stands outside a white society which little suspects his talent, but who understands tribal and human values, which he expresses in his art. Si Johnson's art was expressed in stories about a very small boy who shot bedbugs with a bow and arrow, who when his village was attacked escaped through a knot in the door, who befriended a bird that had assisted him, and so on. The physically weak outsider with special powers which allowed him or her to stand out against the dominant culture was a familiar story to Hope, who over the years had studied Richard Rolle, those for whom the *Ancrene Riwle* was written, and now Margery Kempe.

In 1935 she had mentioned, almost in passing, a story she had heard from Mrs. Sarah Powis, whom she described as an "Iroquois women of the Oneida Tribe" in an article she published in the *Journal of American Folklore*. It concerned a wren whose song shook the twig he was perched upon: "See what a great bird I am," he said. "I shake the world." Hope had presented the story to show "the character of the wren as it can be observed from life," which she thought might "help to explain the European designation of the bird as 'Little King.'" In 1944 she published in the same journal "An Oneida Tale," a story told to her by Lydia Doxtader (who had died in 1926), the aunt of Anna Johnson and the daughter of William Doxtader (Billy Birchtree), all of whom Hope had known. The story concerned the search of Beans for food to sustain him, and his rejection of an owl (who will only give him snakes and mice to eat), and a frog (who offers worms and flies), in favor of Corn, and the story accounts for the practice of planting corn and beans together, so the beans can climb the corn as they grow.

In her notes to the brief story Hope noted the five times from March or April, 1917, through February 28, 1919, and another unspecified period of time when she had gathered narratives of the tribe, primarily from members of the same family. In her last years she returned to this material and published some of it. Later still, in the 1950s, she took a keen interest in archaeological digging that was undertaken in the tribal grounds, but in her publications she seems also to have been preserving something of her own encounters with a tribe and a family whom she had come to know and to esteem, and who she knew were in danger of being forgotten.

During her last years in Oneida her interest in politics quickened, and like most of Hope's other nonmedieval interests, it had family origins. By 1932 the family member to whom she was closest was her brother Grosvenor, then chief of design at the Oneida factory. His wife, Christine Hapgood Hamilton (1875–1952), was also a child of the community and like Hope had been educated in Niagara Falls but had gone to college at Mt. Holyoke. Christine was keenly interested in social causes, having majored in education and subsequently become a social worker. Later she became influential in the New York League of Women Voters and helped Mrs. Eleanor Roosevelt organize Democratic women in New York State. Having been an alternate to the 1928 Democratic National Convention, she had a real if political friendship with Mrs. Roosevelt. Indeed, she and her husband were visiting Mrs. Roosevelt when the president died. By then Christine's daughter Harriett, whom Hope had escorted to Europe in 1929, was active in the Roosevelt wing of the Democratic party. Hope was not particularly close to her sister-in-law, but her interest in familial affairs, her attachment to her neice, and her rapidly developing concern for economic and world affairs brought the Roosevelt era into focus for her. Instinctively conservative and rather inclined to discount the devastating effect of the Depression in America, Hope knew that the period of American isolation was over, and, concerned as she was for the fate of Britain, she did not regret its passing.

Another interest that deepened during the war was Russia, and that interest also had personal connections. Her initial connections were through the Herberts, whose daughter was married to the Soviet envoy in London, but as the war progressed, she recalled other associations: she had known two Russian students at Newnham, and had long been a reader of Russian fiction. On February 20, 1943, she wrote an unfinished five-page single-spaced memorandum (now in Oxford) in which she recalled these and other associations, including a meeting with Anna Louise Strong during an Atlantic crossing in 1936, though she may also have met her in 1904, during an unhappy year Strong spent at Bryn

Mawr. Hope's impressions were somewhat unconnected, but she believed that the Russian revolution had brought much good, and recalled
that certain Soviet teachings were anticipated in Christianity. "Whatsoever you give to the least of my little ones you give unto me," she noted,
had implications for Communist as well as for Christian theory.

Her memorandum was going to continue with thoughts about the
North African landings, which were taking place about the time she was
writing. In it she was probably going to support British interests in the
face of American liberal opinion which distrusted British intentions, and
she believed that her sympathy towards some aspects of the Soviet Union
thus presented a balanced political outlook, since what she had written
would not please some of her more conservative friends. But her commitment to the Allied cause was total. There are memories of her even today
in Oneida sitting rigidly attentive to the radio, listening to the war reports
from London. On January 20, 1945, she wrote to Day (in a letter now in
Oxford):

> Though a Roosevelt voter, I have lately taken the Herald-Tribune – for
> thus I see [Walter] Lippmann – and the library here takes only the Times,
> and our local papers do not carry Lippmann – as did those of Ann Arbor,
> Detroit and Toronto. I think that except for the political editorials for
> [Thomas E.] Dewey the HT is being very fair, and during the campaign
> they carried so much practically for FDR one wondered what was the
> actual state of mind of the staff. Of course Lippman went for FDR finally,
> and [George Fielding] Eliot (the military writer) said the day after the
> election that he was relieved. I sent you some batches of special articles –
> columns, etc. – a mixed lot. I think I also sent you poor [Wendell L.]
> Willkie – but I would never have wanted him to be president for with all his
> fine impulses he did not seem to me to have balance in emergencies – even
> common men might have more.

During the war Hope kept in touch with American editors who were
working on the various versions of the *Ancrene Riwle*. In 1940 she visited
in Philadelphia her old friend Albert Baugh, who was at work on one of
the English versions. His wife remembers the visit and how, after a long
discussion in which Hope liberally provided detail after detail to assist
with the editing, he privately suggested to her that she take Hope for a
walk so that he could set down on paper what she had said. The incident
is a good example of the sort of help Hope gave those whose interests and

persons she approved. Her conversation, though not exactly random and never misguided, was quick and allusive, tending to frequent shifts and moving from recondite and learned to more homely matters.

Earlier she had advised Charlotte D'Evelyn in London and put her in touch with experts in the British Museum; D'Evelyn's EETS edition of the Latin version appeared in 1944, the same year that Herbert's edition of the French text was published, dedicated to Hope.

Baugh's edition appeared in 1956, Day's (Based on Herbert's transcription) in 1952, R. M. Wilson's in 1954, and W. H. Trethewey's in 1958. Trethewey, an Anglo-Norman scholar in the University of Toronto, had been recommended by Germaine Dempster, the Chaucerian textual critic, during a visit to Oneida when Dempster had excused herself from the task by pleading a limited knowledge of Anglo-Norman. Hope worked closely with Trethewey, and she even referred to him as a "collaborator," also remarking his courtesy and his excellent work. In the end the published edition was Trethewey's alone, though he paid generous tribute to Hope's assistance and encouragement, and their relationship stands in sharp contrast to her earlier association with Sanford Meech.

There is evidence among Hope's papers that she advised and encouraged the editors of all these editions, except Wilson's, providing what she knew and helping make contacts to establish what she did not. Two years after her death Tolkien's edition appeared, and it too she had encouraged respectfully and at a distance. If a scholar's contribution is to be measured not only by work produced but also by work encouraged, Hope's contribution by no means ended in 1940. The proliferation of editions of *Ancrene Riwle* editions owed much to her efforts.

After the war ended, Hope did not return to Britain, though as late as the early 1950's she all but promised to do so in her correspondence. During the war her never-robust health deteriorated. On April 6, 1944, she wrote to Mabel Day: "The truth is that ever since I came home from the war I have been feeling exceedingly the long pent-up strain of the years when I worked on the dictionary plus MK and especially the difficult years after 1935." The struggle with Sanford Meech took its toll, and a fall she suffered about 1950 further contributed to her debility. Thus her reasons for not returning to Britain were largely physical, but as the years wore on, they may also have been influenced by concern about what she would find on her return. Her place in the house on Cheyne

Walk, which she had signed back to Marietta Pallis, had been taken by a mutual friend, and it would not have been easy for Hope to find a new home. The friend died in 1955, but Hope was by then too ill to return. Hope and Marietta thereafter all but split because of Hope's reluctance, in Marietta's eyes, to show sympathy for the death, but it is possible to understand Hope's reasons.

On March 24, 1946, Dorothy Ellis wrote Hope a letter (now in Oxford) which suggested how postwar Britain was changing, and which also showed the strength of character with which Dorothy was confronting the changes :

> I seem to have got completely out of touch with all our old happy life and interests, except that I still have my war-time seat on the British Records Preservation Section Committe and so see Joan [Wake] from time to time. She is a tower of strength in a shifting world. I am feeling rather lost in a way, because now I do not think it will ever be possible for me to get back to medieval interests; for one thing I am too much tied up with the material things Skagie [Skay] used to do for me. This is not entirely a grumble by the way—I've become a most domestic person: I bottle fruit extremely well, and I brought Aunt Sarah a jar of chutney which I made from an American recipe out of a book which a G.I. gave me. It is very good indeed. Did you ever meet my Georgiana? We haven't any maids who live in the house now, but Georgiana, whom I have known for more than thirty years (she is nearly fifty) is the most devoted friend, and she was very, very fond of Skagie [Skay].
>
> Incidentally she is a very good cook. . . . Both Charles and David the chauffeur came back safely and came back to me, but I can't afford two men at the present rates, and David, who married during the war, has gone to a job where he and his wife could have a flat. He was with me for four months and did a lot of good work about the rather dilapidated house— pointing, and so on—and he got the old car done up beautifully and fit for the road. . . .

Dorothy's letter is virtually an essay on social change in postwar Britain, showing her awareness that many of the alterations that were not to her advantage, were nevertheless for the best.

Hope's desire to return to England never faded, even when her health made the journey impossible. After a lapse in the correspondence, Dorothy wrote with apologies, and on June 9, 1952, Hope wrote a letter (now in Oxford) in reply:

> My dearest Dorothy,
>
> I am sure you never gave greater plesaure by a letter than with the one to me just received. But how could you ever say to me that you had been 'ashamed' to write? Surely we went years ago beyond all such considerations – taking each other's contingencies realistically – knowing that existed underneath – I am deeply grateful for your affection and if I don't think of our happy times too much it is because it makes me sad to do so since – though I insist as to not being sure as to this – I know it will be hard for me to go over again – I appear to be a very old lady.

But not one who has given up. In the same letter she insists that her arthritis, thanks to weekly injection, is "not very painful" and that she continues to do "my daily bit on BMK II."

Increasingly the direction of that volume shifted. Hope's plan for the book was initially based on the source book for the *Ancrene Riwle* which she had been projecting. It was not to be a study from her hand alone, not a collection of notes gathered subsequent to volume one. Rather it would contain long excerpts from works which she believed bore importantly on Margery's world. Many of the works she identified, like *The Chastising of God's Children*, *The Orchard of Syon*, and *The Mirror of Simple Souls*, have now been published, and it would be superfluous to reissue them. But during the 1950s her interests were moving in two directions, touching on the questions of Suso's influence, and the impact of Rhineland spirituality in Britain on the one hand, and the nature and direction of the native mystical tradition on the other. In this second question she was concerned to treat the interconnection between the *Ancrene Riwle* and what she came to see as the continuity of English mysticism, a continuity she believed was changed markedly by a number of late-medieval English translations.

During this period Hope rethought her attitude toward the *Book of Margery Kempe*, and toward mysticism generally. In the past her formulations had always been precise: Richard Rolle was a mystic, and texts either were or were not from his hand, a judgment which depended on, among other things, the nature of the mysticism they were taken to reveal. The judgment she was accustomed to make reached back to the example of Mary Berenson, but now she was conditioned by her work on the *Ancrene Riwle,* and on the localization and circulation of manuscripts, fields in which she had worked for many years. Radical empiricist she remained, but she began to modify what she had thought and even what she had published. Speaking of her early work on the origin of the *Ancrene Riwle,* she noted in a November 4, 1945, letter to Dr. Day that "I would now put the Kilburn theory much more doubtfully," and as the decade advanced, she moved away from the identification of persons to the identification of attitudes.

The difficulty with this process was that, although her ideas changed, her language did not. She still used the categories she had adopted in her examination of Rolle, still followed the convention of designating as "mystical" a whole range of devout practices. The result is that her vocabulary can seem rather more broad and her thinking less precise than they in fact were. During her last twenty years in Oneida she extended her thinking into areas which had interested her before, feminism, devotion, mysticism, but which she had earlier treated separately. Now she was emboldened to consider their mutual implications, and thus the term "mysticism" became less absolute. She applied it easily to Margery, since she wished to counter those critics who dismissed Margery as a "hysteric"; and though she agreed that Margery showed hysterical elements in her personality, she insisted too that a new convention was developing. She was also inclined to allow that Margery was influenced greatly by the changing devotional practices around her, as Richard Rolle was not, and became disposed to see Margery's spirituality less as the product of a single person than as the product of a series of new practices. Thus the *Book* became a kind of anti-Lollard document, but one which also bore a relationship to the earlier and more moderate spirituality of the *Ancrene Riwle.* The differences between these traditions she sought to account for by remarking the influence of Rhineland mysticism, so creating what she came to call the divided tradition of "English contemplative piety." One characteristic of this piety was that it was not mystical, as she had used the term before, though it now embraced the teachings of such mystics as Saint Bridget of Sweden.

Retaining the language of mysticism, language that would command respect and attention, she moved toward a volume which would be like the collection of related texts such as she had contemplated for the *Ancrene Riwle,* but with a difference. This book would be concerned less with the tradition the work had created than with the complex two-dimensional tradition it drew upon.

But time does not draw all things to completion, and in the end Hope had to leave this project for other hands. She lived only to see the beginning of what she hoped for. Between 1940 and 1960 a number of scholars became active in a field that earlier had been hers, and that of a few friends, alone. Texts like *The Chastising of God's Children* or *The Orchard of Syon* were reserved, often with but sometimes without Hope's approval. It thus no longer made sense to quote long sections of a text which would shortly appear in its entirety or to quote continental works, except in Middle English translation. But subsequent publications have not always completed or even addressed the problems Hope would have raised. Take, for example, the first volume of *The Orchard of Syon*, published in 1966 as volume 258 of the Early English Text Society, edited by Phyllis Hodgson and Gabriel Liegey. Hope had encouraged the editors to undertake the task, a fifteenth-century English translation of *The Dialogue* of Saint Catherine of Siena, since with St. Bridget and Walter Hilton, Catherine was one of the three most widely read new authors. The translation was probably undertaken for the use of the nuns of Syon Abbey, in whom Hope was, as we have seen, greatly interested. But the exact connection with Syon, and so with the fifteenth-century English religious tradition, remains unstudied, at least in part becasue the second volume of the EETS edition has not appeared. Further study of *The Orchard* would undoubtedly examine not only the historical allusions which interested Hope in her early years but also the links between the older mystical traditions and the new practices which engaged her later years. Thus for example, Saint Catherine of Siena was one of the continental mystics whose ability to speak and write about her experiences and whose active role in promoting her revelations Hope credited with playing a part in changing the religious climate of fifteenth-century England.

These texts confirmed Hope's belief in the importance of women to the emerging contemplative tradition. Against what some scholars, like G. G. Coulton, took to be the failed idealism of the Middle Ages, Hope placed the tough-minded integrity of those who, despising social convention, followed the demanding enclosed life of the spirit. Although men also followed that life, to Hope it appeared that with women its values emerged most clearly, as if the more enthusiastic, more ecstatic practices were the ones which mattered most. And since it was for women that many of the mystical works were translated, it was they who joined the new Continental practices to the more restrained English tradition. For evidence of this new tradition she turned, urged on by the *Book of Margery Kempe*, to Saint Bridget of Sweden, and from there to Syon Abbey. She also studied Meister Eckhart (ca. 1260–1327), John Tauler (ca. 1300–1361) Henry Suso (ca. 1295–1366), Gertrude (1232–1291) and her younger sister Mechtild (1241–1299) of Hackeborn, Mechtild of Magdeburg (1207–1282) and others associated with her convent, and Hildegard of Bingen (ca. 1098–1179). These devout persons, together with Saint Catherine and St. Bridget, would identify the parameters of the new tradition she sought to define. Most scholars now follow Hope in believing that German and Flemish mystical texts deeply influenced British devotion in the fifteenth century, though not all would agree that transmission came in part through those working in the wool trade with the low countries, many of whom were resident in London.

A good deal of evidence now points to the influence of religious houses, including those of the Carthusians whose influence has been much studied. But there is a subtext to the more recent insistence on Carthusian transmission from which Hope would have dissented: for it is sometimes implied that personal devotions (and what are called "foreign heresies") were made orthodox by the circumstances of their tansmission through religious houses, but Hope was sensitive to the way in which "mystical" devotions flourished without reference to ecclesiastical permission, and responded not only to the orderly doctrines so pleasing to the scholar, but also to each other, and to the sometimes disorderly circumstances of religious life. The short memorandum of her conversation with Hope that Helen Gardner wrote in July, 1939, begins: "Margery Kempe's inspiration was probably German movement, which was feminist, hysterical & visionary. German women mystics were connected with Dominicans; who were strong in Norwich." The German, visionary and feminist themes reappear in the appendices she contributed to the EETS edition of the *Book of Margery Kempe*, but these were only the beginning.

Continental, particularly German, devotions she expected to show in the second volume of that edition had been humanized in their English adoption. The less demonstrative native strain was the product of devout women both famous and unknown; and at the head of this tradition, which emphasized silence and an absence of external activity, stood the *Ancrene Riwle*. In asserting the humane dimension to this native tradition, Hope intended more than a general description, and one very interesting example may have been intended to show one atypical result of the confrontation of the new practices and the established tradition. One section of the book was to treat the close but almost certainly platonic friendship between Joanna Sewell, a fifteenth-century Bridgittine nun at Syon Abbey, and James Grenehalgh, a Carthusian scholar and scribe at the Charterhouse at Sheen, just across the Thames. Hope's interest in their relationship (which resulted in Grenehalgh leaving Sheen for another charterhouse) was well known to a small group of scholars whom she consulted, and indeed her interest in it seems to have gone back at least to 1915. Hope's correspondence (now at Bryn Mawr) with the distinguished Oxford paleographer Neil Ker contains a detailed treatment of the topic, including remarks on the dramatic monogram of linked names which appears in some manuscripts, and the heartfelt notes in drypoint by Grenehalgh renouncing his love which appear in others. But the love of the two religious, deeply rooted in a shared devotion to the love of God, was not general knowledge, and the careful discussion she intended for the second volume of the *Book of Margery Kempe* would undoubtedly have had the impact she anticipated.

The project that emerged was thus a large one and might well have required a lifetime to complete, and if in her last years of failing health Hope came to understand that she would not bring her book to completion, she saw, as Joan Wake said, that the task would be taken up by other hands. The detail she required did not allow the scholar to work quickly. But she had precipitated much of what was to come.

It is important to remember that throughout her life Hope wrote from what she referred to on March 12, 1949, in a letter to C. T. Onions (now in Oxford) as "my state of 'Christian agnosticism.'" Freed from the necessity of distinguishing between those works which show response to a divine presence and those which give evidence of devotion and piety, she moved easily from text to text, taking her direction from the quality of mind and the kind of sensibility she knew to be at work. Yet there is in her late work the implication that the values she observes are those which historically had attached themselves more often to women than to men.

Increasingly, there was in her work a response to scholars like Coulton who emphasized too much the limitations of medieval civilization. The values she studied, those of recluses, stood somehow outside that civilization, Hope implied, yet they were paradoxically at its very center. Her knowledge of manuscripts led her to note that the works of Rolle, Walter Hilton, and others often circulated together among the same intellectual and spiritual communities. The importance of these texts for women, she felt, was great, particularly since after 1066 silence, not speech, became what was required of them. England, unlike the Continent, had produced no women scholars, few authors, and still fewer prominent spirtiual leaders. Since 1066 no Englishwoman had been canonized. Only in devout religion, then, did women find a voice. Accustomed by long residence in Oneida to recognize how heroic strength of character can find an outlet in religious practice, accustomed to attaching more importance to that character than to the points of dogma which gave it birth, she saw a continuity in English religious life which she believed her texts both reflected and produced. In the fifteenth century a new strain of spirituality arose, she believed, which gave the lie to the silent centuries that had gone before.

This new tradition she believed, was more expressive, more visionary, but was in certain important ways like the larger tradition from which it had emerged. Its new German and feminist components were changed in its English setting, and the nature of the connections between the two Hope was still investigating at the time when she had to suspend work more than a year before her death. She noted that it was Dom Butler's "vision, locution, and revelation" which characterized the new tradition, most of the practitioners of which had been women. She noted too the group of women Thurston had observed around the French noblewoman Marie d'Oignies (ca. 1177–1213), who like Margery had obtained her husband's consent to undertake an ascetic and celibate life, and whose biography, in Middle English translation, she understood to be connected to the new tradition. She thought that the group had been influenced by some of Rolle's texts, though Rolle himself she took to be representative of the earlier tradition. In Julian of Norwich Hope had discovered an elevated conflict between the two traditions, and Julian's *Revelations* she thought responded to both; focused in scope and attitude in a way

Margery Kempe never was, Julian equally embraced the new, more ecstatic tradition.

In all of this she allowed a greater role to the devotional tradition than she had before, and she insisted that women were a major factor directing its development. She also saw an element of protest: women were, in their devotions, articulating a degree of freedom of expression that had been denied them by the social circumstances in which they lived. For this insight, the experience with the EETS edition of Margery Kempe was perhaps partly responsible, but she saw too how the phenomena she continued to call mysticism had moved out of the oratory and into a larger world. She would not have added "transforming it," but it is possible to believe that some such larger possibility would have emerged as she ordered her book. The role of contemplation and of piety in spreading mystical texts she took to be central, and she would not have been surprised to discover devotional as well as mystical elements in the *Book of Margery Kempe*. It depends, she might have said, on how you define your terms. She herself defined "mysticism" with a certain latitude and attached to it an element of feminism she had earlier associated exclusively with the *Ancrene Riwle*. Her approach was not altogether orthodox, but it was a major reformulation of the terms in which late medieval English spirituality had been cast.

During the time she was at work on the volume, she kept in touch with her friends in Britain. On January 7, 1954, Dorothy Ellis wrote that she had seen Joan Wake at a Records Association Conference in December and that she was recovering from a blow:

> I had last heard from her just after her niece was killed in that frightful point-to-point [a cross-country horse competition] and she was then depressed by growing old as well as by everything else. Now she was even more her old self than in the best of the old days—happy and gay, full of kindly delightful malice and rejoicing in her book: and no wonder: I have been reading it with quite breathless admiration and pleasure—that is the way to make history come alive.

The book Dorothy referred to was *The Brudenells of Deene*, on which Joan had been working for years, a bright and informal family history which had come from her work on Northampton's local history. Hope saw Joan in April, 1957, when she visited America to lecture on British local history at Milton Academy and Emmanuel College, and to visit North-ampton, Massachusetts. Joan described her nine week visit in an article in *Northamptonshire Past and Present*, where she mentions briefly her visits to Oneida at the beginning and end of her trip. But in Hope's Oxford papers there are references to the meetings with Hope which suggest that these visits were virtually the reason for the trip. What she found was not comforting. By 1957 Hope's arthritis was advanced, and she was within eighteen months of suspending work forever.

An earlier Oneida visitor was G. G. Coulton, her old mentor from Cambridge and her continuing supporter, whom she kept as a friend but from whom she kept a certain distance. In May, 1942 he visited her in Oneida and in the course of things discussed the original community. Coulton, as usual, proposed objections. His letter of thanks for the visit is of interest, since it gives a last insight into Hope's regard for the institution to which she had been attached since birth. Writing from Toronto on May 22 (the letter is now at Bryn Mawr), Coulton allowed that Oneida

> helped me a little more to realize the possible dignity & humanistic culture of a society owing little or nothing to the "domestic servant" class.
>
> I must also say one word about our Sat. night talk. Your generous point of view, and your plain earnest rebuke of my "legalisms," impressed me even on the points where it left me unconvinced. After all, God made us to agree to differ, or He wouldn't have made us so different.

During World War II Hope had come to know the Norwegian novelist Sigrid Undset, two years her senior, who visited Oneida almost every year during her wartime exile in America. Sigrid Undset had attracted attention with her novel *Kristin Lavransdatter*, set in fourteenth-century Norway and published in three volumes between 1920 and 1922. Al-though it had appeared in an English translation in 1930, Hope had not read it, though she seems to have known that Undset had won the Nobel Prize in literature in 1928. Undset's themes were both moral and re-ligious; she had converted to Catholicism in 1924 and she was particularly concerned with the problems faced by women, another trait that would have commended her to Hope, who also admired her academic cast of mind and her attention to detail. The two discussed the *Book of Margery Kempe*, about which Sigrid wrote an article in *Atlantic Monthly* in 1939, and their correspondence continued until Sigrid's death in 1949.

A third visitor was Lady Ruth Darwin, whom Hope had met through Dorothy Ellis. She came to Oneida in the 1950s and stayed in Mansion House, visiting with Hope and walking in the nearby hills. In a 1958 letter (now in Oneida) Lady Ruth recalled meeting an old man picking apples who called to his wife to come out and see "the grandaughter of the infernal Darwin." The man later produced a collection of fossils which he believed disproved her grandfather's theories.

Other connections that Hope continued and developed were more complicated, particularly the academic ones. In one instance she came to believe, wrongly as it transpired, that a conscientious and perceptive student whom she had assisted had benefited from her work but was not disposed to acknowledge her discoveries properly. It is much to her credit that Hope was able to see that she had been in error and subsequently assisted the young scholar in publication.

One attack that Hope faced late in her life was real enough, though it has a somewhat tangled history. A mistake she had made in her study of Rolle was picked up a decade later by E. J. F. Arnould, a lecturer in French in the University of Manchester and later a professor in Trinity College, Dublin. He had earlier pointed out a slip in one of her articles on Anglo-Norman. In "Richard Rolle and a Bishop: A Vindication," published in the the April, 1937, issue of the *Bulletin of the John Rylands Library*, Arnould indicated pointedly that an identification Hope had sought to make was almost certainly in error. Referring to a fourteenth-century controversy in which he had become engaged, Richard Rolle had written, with amused irony, of his younger self: "Ecce juvenis... insurgit contra senem, heremita contra episcopus" [Behold the youth... rises against the old man, the hermit against the bishop] and Hope, like others before her, had taken the reference to mean that the zealous young hermit had opposed himself to an elderly bishop. But Arnould reasonably pointed out that the bishop in question was, from the context of the passage, almost certainly Saint Anselm, who lived in the twelfth century and was not a fourteenth-century contemporary, and that the real issue was the primacy which Rolle, in his youth, felt that the solitary held over the monastic community.

This interpretation rendered superfluous Hope's efforts to identify, from a contemporary document, the bishop in question. Arnould's intervention was entirely appropriate, though it is possible to believe from his tone that he was making the most of the matter, perhaps, as others have done since, to establish his own authority by indicating a slip in Hope's by now authoritative oeuvre. The difficulty was that in his article he had quoted a number of long passages from two manuscripts of Rolle's *Melos amoris* with which he had been working, and these transcriptions contained very many errors. In a subsequent study of Rolle which appeared in the April, 1940, issue of the *Revue d'ascétique et de mystique*, Dom Wilmart noted Arnould's study and also the errors it contained in terms which seem unusually severe. More than a decade later, when Arnould was seeking Hope's support for an edition of the *Melos* which he had completed, she twice brought Wilmart's remarks to his attention, having other and she believed, better scholars in mind for the work. The correspondence between the two, preserved at Bryn Mawr, is unusually sharp and may reasonably account for the attack on Hope and her work which appears in Arnould's 1957 edition of the *Melos*.

On yet another occasion she believed that a younger scholar had been careless and somewhat discourteous, and probably too that he was moving into areas that were beyond him. In the last two cases in particular, no doubt her experience with Meech disposed her to protest and take exception as she would not have in the past, and she seems to have felt too senior and accomplished to be patronized or dismissed by younger male colleagues. She may not have been right in all of her apprehensions, but neither was she always mistaken.

With her academic friends of long standing, however, her relationships continued to flourish. Her correspondence with Oliger, discontinued during the war, began again soon afterward, and it continued until his death in 1951. She also renewed her contacts with Kenneth Sisam, C. T. Onions, Dorothy Everett, Helen Gardner, and Phyllis Hodgson, and through the last three she had some influence in designating editors for EETS editions. Gardner became better known for her work on metaphysical poets in the 1950s and 60s than for her early work on Walter Hilton's *The Ladder of Perfection*, which she had originally intended to edit but on whose first rung, she later joked, she had broken a leg. Still, her early work on Hilton was as promising as her later work on the metaphysicals was to prove, and after her appointment to St. Hilda's College, Oxford, in 1941, she became associated with a group of women, including Dorothy Everett, Phyllis Hodgson, and, less actively, Mabel Day, who met separately among themselves and were concerned with vetting EETS editions, particularly those touching on or associated with the *Ancrene Riwle*.

With this group Hope's influence was active, but it was not as effective as it had been before the war. The earlier academic and personal communications with Gardner, for example, gave way to letters concerning the assignment of appropriate editors for EETS volumes, and in this process Hope felt that she had an official interest, both because she wished to encourage the appointment of certain competent American editors and because she believed that she spoke with some authority on matters touching the *Ancrene Riwle*. Everett kept her informed of the assignments the group made and attended to her advice. No doubt the miles between Oneida and Oxford lessened the effectiveness of certain of her counsels, but she was still able to support editors whom she believed able. By the late 1950s her direct influence had diminished, partly as a result of the increasingly sharp though consistently courteous tenor of her suggestions and corrections, particularly those addressed to Gardner and Hodgson. With Gardner there arose a misunderstanding over the designation of an EETS editor, which neither could control, though both could influence. With Hodgson she held a pointed discussion concerning the notes to Hodgson's edition of *The Cloud of Unknowing*, and the two had a disagreement over a passage which Hope insisted in a letter of July 26, 1956 (now at Bryn Mawr) was a warning against certain "fantastic late medieval devotions" current in the period. By the next year her health had curtailed Hope's correspondence.

Through the years Hope kept her eye on the development of the editions of the *Ancrene Riwle*. On August 31, 1945, she wrote to Mabel Day:

> I feel almost at rest about giving over MK if AR is to be printed instead — whereas I should have felt very low if you brot out now some indifferent texts. I am glad the Council sees how important it is to get on with AR in the lifetime of inured enthusiasts — Prof. Chambers, alas, is gone, Dr. Flower is failing, I fear, but the Oxford group remain, and I feel Dr. Onions will prefer this to other work.

She established contact with a number of younger British scholars, including Neil Ker and Ian Doyle, and during her last twenty years she both sought and gave advice. Paul Grossjean, S.J., the Bollandist, stayed in contact with her, but to W. A. Pantin she confided on May 22, 1956, "I am sure you miss Dom Wilmart as much as I do." To Mabel Day she sent a stream of letters both academic and increasingly, personal. When her old Bryn Mawr friend Charlotte D'Evelyn met F. M. Powicke in 1949, he especially asked to be remembered to Hope, and such greetings, however conventional, gave her much satisfaction. Meech was now chairman of the Department of English in Syracuse University. He and Hope met in passing, sometimes, at MLA meetings in New York.

Among the tasks that she began during this time was her response to a review of the *Book of Margery Kempe* by the Catholic historian E. I. Watkin which appeared in the *Downside Review* in July, 1941. The review troubled her less for its criticisms than because she felt that it, and a later anonymous review in the *Tablet* on August 23 of the same year, somewhat misrepresented her position. She wrote to Watkin early in 1944 when the review came to her attention (an unusually large number of drafts are preserved at Bryn Mawr), with a feeling of surprise rare in her correspondence; evidently the direction of the attack took her by surprise, perhaps even hurt her. Watkin had set himself to defend Margery against the attack he believed was implied in some of Hope's notes and in the edition as a whole. Hope's position was that she had been defending Margery against the contempt in which some scholars held her, insisting on what she called the "mystical" element in her *Book*, though not denying a "hysterical" element in her personality.

But Watkin was not prepared to allow any such sentiment to detract from what were to him the work's advantages, and his remarks put Hope in a quandary. She was prepared to see a nonrational dimension to the *Book*, and even allow for a degree of "hysteria" (the word had been legitimated in a series of academic articles in the 1920s), which, however, she thought did not finally detract from it, but she was concerned that she might be misunderstood in Catholic circles. "The extraordinary thing," she wrote, "is I supposed I might be accused of special pleading on Margery's behalf. I dare say I shall be, when my whole 'synthesis' is in print." She believed that she had shown no "malice" toward mysticism in her contributions to volume 1, and she insisted that her purpose in "scrutinizing mystical phenomena" was not far from Watkins's own purpose, and she would, she said, write a supplement to his article rather than a rejoinder. Margery was for her a "minor mystic," as she would show in volume 2.

Watkin had evidently written to her twice (I have not been able to trace the letters), and she wrote that she was

> glad to have your comments, and [I] hope that in the later discussion of MK in my general Introduction I shall be able to make my own opinion clearer to you than I did in my notes. I do not blame MK – and pity her only because she obviously could not always act as she wished to. As you say, in the larger sense she is not to be pitied, quite the reverse. But I feel you judge her (if I may say so) from the somewhat aloof vantage point of centuries later – the historian has to concern him or her self with conditions of the time – as did contemporaries like the author of the *Cloud* – who from observations had evidently seen the movement beginning which culminated in Elizabeth Barton. He could not judge the matter in a vacuum with philosophical "fairness" – tho even he probably knew that vagaries like M's had co-existed with heights of spirituality. What he saw was that a sort of infection of sensualised mysticism was creeping over English devotion he *felt* from the point of view of the tradition embodied in the *Ancrene Riwle*, as it seems to me. I do not think it was an accident that only the ethical St. Bridget had real popularity in 15th century England, of the women mystics, when translated. A whole difference in national tradition was in question – such a difference as can be appreciated by reading the group of the German Dominican women altogether.

The letter contains one of her clearest statements about her own feelings toward Margery and toward the kind of spirituality she believed that Margery embodied. She remained, she said, personally sympathetic towards Margery and yet felt she could not be understood apart from the larger devotional traditions of her time. Individual attitudes toward Margery herself Hope implies, are beside the point. What matters more is that she should be understood in context.

Hope's reference to Saint Bridget is particularly interesting, for it alludes to the last great interest of her life, one that had begun years earlier. Saint Bridget of Sweden (ca. 1303–1373) married at the age of thirteen, had eight children (Saint Catherine of Sweden being one of them), and founded an order of men and women who lived separately but worshiped together. The order is given to poverty except that the members may possess books. As we have seen, years earlier Hope had visited Syon Abbey in Devon, the English mother house of the order. It was at Syon that the manuscript of the *Book of Margery Kempe* had first been preserved, and Hope suspected that the roots of the newer spirituality were to be found there. A lifelong admirer of Syon, she valued her association with this serious and scholarly community of women to the end of her life.

If she would not oppose a critic like Watkin who wrote, as his title said, "In Defense of Margery Kempe," neither would she ignore the challenge to traditional devotional attitudes which Margery's ecstasy occasioned. With such study and such reservation she maintained her academic life even as her health declined, and as trips to libraries became increasingly taxing.

Hope's last years in Oneida were happy ones. The community of the Mansion House held her in high regard and realized that she was a formidable yet approachable scholar, and one who had made a name in the larger world. Stories about her last years are still told there. Those who knew her as children recall how she gathered them together and taught them the history of the community. She sometimes puzzled the younger children: one member recalled seeing her, in her apartment, thrusting her head into a machine with lights and a whining motor – a microfilm reader. Another time two boys went into her apartment (at the top of one of the two towers that rise above Mansion House) to capture a cat. They discovered that a paisley scarf of Hope's would make a good parachute, and they launched the unfortunate animal from her window. The cat survived, but the scarf, dragged through the brambles, did not. The next day Hope posted a fierce rebuke on the community bulletin board; it was not the torn scarf she reprehended but the terror inflicted on the cat.

In those last years, and no doubt in earlier ones too, there were probably those who found her difficult, even eccentric, not a "team player." These traits were, as we have seen, part of her public persona. Those who knew her better usually had a very different view. No doubt her English determination to "do things up to a decent standard" sometimes conflicted with an egalitarian American repect for the individual who works to capacity. Oneida tradition held that these two traits went together and that the assumed quality, even superiority, of the Oneida descendants was based on achieved, not inherited, merit. But not everyone shared her belief that there was a standard of excellence that everyone could agree on.

She continued to believe in the possiblility of improvement, particularly of the young. "I am inclined to believe that a really good teacher of argumentation or expository writing is one of the best citizens of the Republic," she wrote to a Mr. Wesson on February 9, 1943, (in a letter now in Oxford). "I would hope that he or she would teach his or her pupils the value of detail. The modern generation in my experience seems to scorn the only element by which truth can be dissected, sinew by sinew and nerve by nerve." She found herself irritated by having Churchill's reference to "the hyena in Mussolini" headlined in the press "Churchill Calls Mussolini a Hyena." With such examples the young would never learn how much language and precision matter. God lives in detail.

In her last years Hope may also have seemed to be rather unbending. She was capable of talking about the importance of family descent in a way that ran rather against the grain. She did not hesitate to criticize the quality of certain colleges some parents chose for their daughters, or that some women did not think of going to college at all. Some of these interventions were not well received, though her concerns were by no means unjustified. During the 1950s the number of American women attending college and entering the academic profession dropped dramatically, and what Hope was seeing in Oneida reflected a national pattern that is only now being reversed. In any event, her standards did not relax at all, and during this period she herself maintained close connections with Mt. Holyoke and Smith.

She is still recalled reading *Speculum*, the journal of the Mediaeval Academy of America, in the community library, and the man who recalls it also remembers being taken aside and told, "Remember, we're Protestants, but it was the Catholic church which kept learning alive for all those centuries during the Middle Ages."

Idiosyncratic she seemed to some, but to those who had the intelligence and self-confidence to appreciate her, her company was a pleasure. One of her closest friends still remembers long walks during which Hope pulled off sweater after sweater as they settled into their stride. She was keenly aware of family backgrounds and family connections, and, at least in part because of her work for the Oneida Community Centennial, she knew the photographs of the founding members and would remark similarities which had been submerged for decades. She grew fond of those who assisted her, and often the feeling was returned. Her pleasure in family, in genealogy, in the countryside which had been hers from youth remained, and in the end it was these, as well as the library, that consoled her.

As late as 1959, Hope was still able to take an interest in new publications. On February 26 of that year she wrote to the Early English Text Society ordering a copy of a recent publication, W. Meredith Thompson's edition of *The Wohunge of Ure Lauerd* (1958), and the new secretary of the society, R. W. Burchfield, who had answered earlier queries about the progress of Hope's second volume, very courteously sent a presentation copy. But the end was approaching. Late in 1959 or early in 1960 she wrote to Norman Davis, director of the society, relinquishing her volume on Margery Kempe. He answered in a letter which I have not found, though its kindness is evident from Hope's last letter to Mabel Day, sent on January 12, 1960 (now in Oxford, misdated 1959). It was written in an almost indistinct hand which Day transcribed for the EETS files, (Joan Wake partially corrected it in 1961). Hope wrote to acknowledge "news of you, on whch followed a most kind and flattering letter from Professor Norman Davis about my giving up work on BMK vol II." She wrote that she was comfortable, though her reading was confined to "the local and NY newspapers, and works [of] Jane Austin in the new editions brought out by Dr. R. W. Chapman." Her scholar's eye for a good edition had not failed.

The last year of her life was 1960. John F. Kennedy was running for the presidency. Missiles were the issue. It seemed a great distance from childhood for this woman born in the reign of Victoria. In her last years she progressively gave over academic work, though her interest in it remained high. It was her body, not her mind, that was failing.

On June 19, Joan Wake appeared again, having flown from England to be with her at the end. She found Hope calm and lucid, attended, as Joan wrote to Dorothy Ellis on a July 8 (the letter is now in Oxford), by her "favorite nephew & his wife & her beloved Flosie (the wonderful wife of her eldest nephew)." For more than a week the two old friends spent time together every day, Joan reading Jane Austin to her.

Hope Emily Allen died on June 30, 1960.

EPILOGUE

Hope Emily Allen was an easy woman to admire. In the ways in which she was unlike her contemporaries she seems most like us, even as her passions recede into memory. Thus all of her concerns relating to women – to the values women attach to religion, and to the way these values stand against social demands – her interest in mysticism, and her own agnosticism are no longer unfamiliar. No longer unfamiliar too are the texts she addressed. She engaged authors and works that were regarded as minor when she began working on them but that she lived to see become part of the canon of English literature, largely because of her efforts and the encouragement she gave others.

But what is still unfamiliar to us is her role as an independent scholar. In an age in which a Ph.D. and some sort of academic affiliation are almost prerequisites for being heard, a scholar who followed her own interests, particularly when those interests were thought to stray from the common undertaking, was likely to arouse suspicion. To a degree this role was related to her gender (academic openings were even fewer and more restricted in the early twentieth century than they are today) and to her health, but to a degree her life was a matter of choice, related, I believe, to the pleasure she took, on a moderate income, in living in Britain. Student of Carey Thomas she may have been and feminist she undoubtedly became, but she evinces no interest in a traditional academic career. One of the advantages of the *Early Modern English Dictionary* was that she could limit her work without much difficulty and undertake most of it alone, in the private research at which she excelled. But it was not so much privacy she valued as independence and the ability to lead her own life, wherever that might be. The founders of Oneida would have understood.

Medieval studies is too complicated a field to say that any one scholar leads it, but Hope Allen was undoubtedly among the first scholars of her generation, and her contributions, both those from her own hand and those she encouraged from others, have left as deep an imprint on the study of Middle English literature as any before or since. It was thanks in no small part to her work that religious and mystical texts came into their own. In time this contribution had important consequences for the study of medieval literary history: Chaucer could no longer be considered an isolated genius, living apart from his age. Langland's relationship to contemporary theology became intelligible. Malory's tragedy, not only his heroism, emerged. These subsequent reevaluations rested on a connected and intelligible view of late medieval English literature of which Hope Emily Allen's work was a part. In this respect her accomplishment rested upon three distinct concerns.

First, she invested time, energy, and money in the study of wills, ownership inscriptions, documents, and other records, which she understood to be important not only for the light they might throw on a major author but also for their help in defining and tracing the intellectual life which flourished in England between the twelfth and the sixteenth centuries. So much of what she established is now widely accepted, that it is easy to forget that she was not only a scholar but also a pioneer. She was indeed interested in the nobility, but the life of any person moved her. This breadth of interest is now widespread in literary, as in historical, studies. But it was not in her time.

Nor was her second great concern, her interest in women. The *Ancrene Riwle*, not Richard Rolle or Margery Kempe, was her intellectual, indeed, her spiritual, home, and she saw not only in it but also in its study something of the humane, demanding, and sympathetic view of things which the study of women's issues involved. Though she was by no means insensitive to the discrimination that professional women faced, her own feminism was itself discriminating, and she never failed to associate herself with the best scholars in her field, regardless of their gender. Her sense of quality took absolute precedence when she addressed women's issues. Her own commitments, including her commitment to women, ran too deep for her to follow any other course.

164

Epilogue

One of these commitments, and her third great concern, was the way in which women, mystics, religious, who were often ignored by scholars, affected the way things were. The course of literary history, by which she seems often to have meant the course of culture, was inextricably bound up with the attitudes, beliefs, and perceptions of those reckoned by some to be weak and ineffectual. Their work, what they did and thought and wrote, constituted the past and informed the present. When she wrote that scholarship and all that it involved were to her what religion was to others, she wrote no more than the truth.

Her manuscript studies, her belief in women, her enlarged sense of the knowable world, her friendships all sprang from a lively concern for understanding the world about her. It is not too much to say that she contributed greatly to the remaking of the study of Middle English literature, widening its canon, deepening its methodology, expanding its significance. To be sure, she was not alone in this undertaking, but her equals were few, and to the end of her life few were American.

In "The American Scholar" Emerson noted the poverty and solitude that were a part of a scholar's life but concluded: "We will walk on our own feet; we will work with our own hands; we will speak our own minds. The study of letters shall be no longer a name for pity, for doubt, and for sensual indulgence." The facts Hope quarried may not have been the platonic ones Emerson called for, but the independence, courage, and self-reliance that he associated with the scholars he sought were hers as well.

Those whom she knew best outlived her. Until her death on August 30, 1963, Marietta Pallis remained at 116 Cheyne Walk and Long Gores, continuing to paint but increasingly interested in her botanical studies. She published at her own expense a number of scientific studies, which tended toward the end of her life to engage her continuing interests in religion and philosophy. She moved away from the Darwinian evolutionary views which she had earlier maintained and toward the end became increasingly interested in the Jesuit theologian Teilhard de Chardin, with whose work she came to sympathize deeply. The year after Hope's death she published a monograph, *The Status of Fen and the Origin of the Norfolk Broads*, which developed her war work and a 1956 study of peat. Her last monograph, *The Species Unit*, was finished as she recorded barely a month past Epiphany, and published on May 29, 1963.

Dorothy Ellis, who was in some ways Hope's closest friend, remained in Newmarket, continuing the myriad of activities that characterized her. She did not return to scholarship after her contribution to the Cambridgeshire volume of the Victoria County History, but she continued her memberships in local archaeological societies and dedicated herself to the county around her, a one-Englander of the old school whose deep-set Conservative philosophy reached out to the poor, the young, the ill. Hope, who felt herself at home in England as she did in no place other than Oneida, saw herself reflected in this woman, whose decency and forthright integrity she shared. Dorothy Ellis died on December 12, 1968, and her funeral filled All Saints' Church in Newmarket.

But Hope's truest English friend was Joan Wake. If Joan had taken much from Hope, her scholarship and her confidence, she had given much too. Like Dorothy, she continued with her learned societies, but, unlike Dorothy she continued to pursue and to encourage local history. The Northampton Historical Society, which she founded in 1920, celebrated its fiftieth anniversary in 1970, and Miss Joan Wake, C.B.E., now with an honorary M.A. from Oxford and an honorary LL.D. from the University of Leicester, was there not only to receive the gratitude of the membership, but also to speak. Anyone who expected fond recollections did not know the woman. Reminding her audience of the history of the society, she insisted that dangers were present still in the County Reorganization Plan, which would remove from Northamptonshire the Borough of Brackley and Brackley Rural District and certain other villages, all of which had been within the shire since the Domesday Book. The society should stand with the county council, she insisted, which was opposing the plan. The issue was not exactly discussed, but a formal vote was taken and a protest sent. Joan Wake died on January 15, 1974, less than six weeks before her ninetieth birthday.

BIBLIOGRAPHICAL NOTE

The scattered and disorganized state of the manuscripts on which this book is based has necessitated a somewhat unusual method of citation. After Hope Allen died in 1960, one of her closest English friends, Joan Wake, set out to preserve what she could of her friend's papers. Having met Hope's family during a visit to Oneida in 1957, she felt free to urge them to find an American repository for the very extensive body of materials in Oneida; she herself would make contact with Hope's friends in Britain and preserve what she could find there.

With the assistance of Dr. Albert Kerr, Hope's family made her library available to certain academic institutions, but her papers posed a problem. Declined by one institution, they were accepted by Bryn Mawr College and placed, with the assistance of Mrs. Nita S. Baugh and Professor Ruth Dean, who acted as executors, in the college archives, though microfilms and a few related papers were deposited in the University of Pennsylvania. Their acceptance by Bryn Mawr was a remarkably far-sighted commitment for a college with limited resources, even for one of its most distinguished graduates. The Bryn Mawr collection consists of seven Hollander boxes, 10.5 feet of professional and some personal correspondence, offprints, drafts of articles, and miscellaneous notes. It is currently stored as received, with only very broad distinctions, some introduced since Hope's death, and not all of those closely observed. There are plans in hand for cataloguing and reorganizing the collection, but at the moment it is not possible to describe the location of any given document with confidence. Thus I have identified certain letters and papers as preserved at Bryn Mawr and have given the names of the senders and the recipients and the dates.

Certain other documents remained with the family in Oneida, and to them the executors also returned certain papers. Although most of the Oneida papers are personal, there are also some professional papers of some importance, including many letters to Hope from Sanford B. Meech and Colonel W. Butler-Bowdon.

Not far away, in Syracuse University Library, is a third collection of interest, in the library's Oneida Collection, box 40, which includes Hope's letters to her family from Bryn Mawr during her undergraduate and graduate years, her ethnographic notes, and a few other papers. These two collections I have described as "Oneida," and "Syracuse," respectively, and have cited materials in them as I have cited items from the Bryn Mawr collection.

Joan Wake's efforts to locate much of Hope's British correspondence proved successful, and all that she could acquire she presented, bound in three scrapbooks, to the Bodleian Library, Oxford, in 1966 and 1967. Their shelf marks are MSS. English Letters c.212 and d.217 and MS. Engl. Misc. c.484. The Bodleian also preserves a letter from Hope to R. W. Hunt, who arranged for the preservation of Joan Wake's scrapbooks. I have cited these letters as I have the others, designated the collection as "Oxford," without reference to the folio to which the item is attached. The scrapbooks are indexed, and in the Oxford collection identification is relatively simple.

The last collection of papers I have referred to is my own, derived from several sources. Chance acquisitions and purchases in Washington, D.C., and in London have been supplemented by gifts. Before her death Hope turned over some of her papers to scholars, and on some of these, since given to me, my work is continuing. I have also received donations from John Cressey, of Dr. Williams' Library, Ruth Dean, and Ian Doyle, among others. Apart from these collections, I have had access to correspondence still in the hands of the recipients: Ruth Dean, Ian Doyle, Mrs. Margaret Ogden, Syon Abbey, and Saint Michael's Abbey, Farnborough, now at Solesmes.

In a few instances I have not cited the location of the collection when I have named a recipient. In those cases all of the cited letters are in the same location, as follows: Hope's correspondence to her family from Bryn Mawr and her ethnographical notes are in Syracuse University Library; all cited letters to Dorothy Ellis and most of those cited to Mabel Day are in Oxford; most of those cited to Sanford Meech are in Oxford, though there are carbons in my collection and elsewhere; Meech's letters to Hope, which I have not quoted, are among the family papers in Oneida.

The main sources for this book have been the manuscript collections I have just identified, but I have also relied on secondary sources in three subject areas: Oneida, Bryn Mawr, and British social history. When necessary and appropriate, I have noted in the text an authority or a source that qualifies or sets in context a larger issue over which I have not wished to delay, but I have kept such references to a minimum, since my purpose here has been to emphasize the contribution made by Hope and a few others of her generation, not the relatively minor corrections of later scholars. Radical empiricists Hope and her contemporaries may have been, and it is possible to note areas of medieval studies that did not greatly engage them; still they all but created the field of Middle English studies and set it on the foundations upon which it still rests.

Bibliographical Note

For the Oneida background I have used two books edited by Constance Noyes Robertson, *Oneida Community: An Autobiography, 1851–1876* (Syracuse, N.Y.: Syracuse University Press, 1970); and *Oneida Community: The Breakup* (Syracuse University Press, 1972); two books by Pierrepont B. Noyes, *My Father's House: An Oneida Boyhood* (New York: Holt, Rinehart & Winston, 1937); and *A Goodly Heritage* (Oneida, N.Y.: Oneida Ltd., Silversmiths, 1958), the second particularly useful for the history of Oneida during the period of Hope Allen's life. Some letters to Hope have been printed in Jesse Catherine Kingsley, *A Lasting Spring*, ed. Jane Kinsley Rich with the assistance of Nelson M. Blake (Syracuse, N.Y.: Syracuse University Press, 1983). I have also consulted Robert Allerton Parker, *A Yankee Saint: John Humphrey Noyes and the Oneida Community* (New York: G. P. Putnam's Sons, 1935); Maren Lockwood Carden, *Oneida: Utopian Community to Modern Corporation* (Baltimore, Md.: Johns Hopkins University Press, 1969); and Lawrence Foster, *Religion and Sexuality: The Shakers, the Mormons, and the Oneida Community* (New York: Oxford University Press, 1981). All family dates are those recorded in John B. Teeple, *The Oneida Family: Genealogy of a Nineteenth-Century Perfectionist Commune* (Oneida, N.Y.: Oneida Community Historical Committee, 1985).

For Bryn Mawr I have had access to the undergraduate publications, particularly *The Lantern*, *Typin o Bob*, and the class yearbooks for the years Hope was there; and to the following works: Cornelia Meigs, *What Makes a College? A History of Bryn Mawr* (New York: Macmillan Co., 1956); Edith Finch, *Carey Thomas of Bryn Mawr* (New York: Harper & Brothers, 1947); Marjorie Housepian Dobkin, ed., *The Making of a Feminist: Early Journals and Letters of M. Carey Thomas* (Kent, Ohio: Kent State University Press, 1979) and Barbara Miller Solomon, *In the Company of Educated Women, A History of Women and Higher Education in America* (New Haven and London: Yale University Press, 1985). Carey Thomas's own writings have been cited from Barbara Cross, ed., *The Educated Woman in America: Selected Writings of Catherine Beecher, Margaret Fuller, and M. Carey Thomas*, Classics in Education, no. 25 (New York: Teachers's College Press, Columbia University, 1965).

On British social history I am indebted to A. J. P. Taylor, *English History, 1914–1945* (New York: Oxford University Press, 1965); John Stevenson, *British Society, 1914–45*, ed. J. H. Plumb, Pelican History of Britain (London: Penguin Books, 1984); Noreen Branson, *Britain in the Nineteen Twenties*, ed. E. J. Hobsbawn, History of British Society (Minneapolis: University of Minnesota Press, 1976); and in particular Paul Carter, *Another Part of the Twenties* (New York: Columbia University Press, 1977); and Frank Costigliola, *Awkward Dominion: American Political, Economic, and Cultural Relations with Europe, 1919–1933* (Ithaca, N.Y.: Cornell University Press, 1984). The details of American and European interests and the quotation from the British ambassador's report of 1921 are taken from Costigliola (p. 81). I have been indebted to Tracey B. Strong and Helene Keyssar, *Right in her Soul: The Life of Anna Louise Strong* (New York: Random House, 1983); Barbara Strachey and Jayne Samuels, eds., *Mary Berenson: A Self-Portrait from her Diaries and Letters* (New York: Norton, 1983); Michael Clanchy, *England and Its Rulers, 1066–1272* (New York: Fontana, 1983); N. Denholm-Young, *The Country Gentry in the Fourteenth Century with Speical Reference to the Heraldic Rolls of Arms* (London: Oxford University Press, 1969); Anthony Goodman, *The Loyal Conspiracy: The Lords Appellant Under Richard II* (London: Routledge & Kegan Paul, 1971); Nigel Abercrombie, *The Life and Work of Edmund Bishop* (London: Longmans, 1959); and J. Bignami Odier; L. Brou, O.S.B.; and A. Vernet, *Bibliographie sommaire des travaux de Pere André Wilmart, O.S.B., 1876–1941*, Sussidi Eruditi 5 (Rome, 1953); and I have also used Dom F. Cabrol's eulogy for the empress Eugénie delivered at Farnborough on July 20, 1920, and published by the abbey. I have used published lifetime tributes and bibliographies for A. G. Little (1939) and Sir William Craigie (1952), in both of which Hope's name appears among the subscribers, and obituaries appearing in scholarly journals, particularly those in *Proceedings of the British Academy* for British scholars, including Flower (1946), Craigie (1961), and Sisam (1972), and in *Speculum* for the Americans. I have also had recourse to occasional publications of the various public and academic bodies to which I have referred. The Society for Pure English published its early history and list of members in its first SPE tract, *Preliminary Announcement* (1919), and I have also used Craigie's "Study of American English," which appeared as tract 27 (1927). I have used J. H. Sondheimer, *History of the British Federation of University Women, 1907–1957* (London, 1957), and a number of current guides and guidebooks for Crosby Hall, Battersea Parish Church, Syon House, and Saint Margaret's Church, Barking. I have had further assistance from friends and colleagues, which I have recorded in the foreword.

THE WORKS OF HOPE EMILY ALLEN

The following list excludes undergraduate publications and letters to the editor printed in newspapers, journals, and magazines published outside London. Periodical abbreviations are those of *PMLA*.

1910

"The Authorship of the *Prick of Conscience*." In *Studies in English and Comparative Literature Presented to Agnes Irwin, Litt.D., Dean of Radcliffe College, 1894–1909*. Radcliffe College Monograph Series, no. 15. Boston: Ginn and Co., pp. 115–70.

1911

"*The Desert of Religion*: Addendum." *Archiv für das Studium der neueren Sprachen und Literaturen* 187:338–91.

1912

"A Note on Tennyson's 'Morte D'Arthur.'" *MLR* 7:99–100.

1913

"Richard Rolle's 'Incendium Amoris'" [letter]. *Athenaeum*, August 23, p. 184.

1916

"Two Middle English Translations from the Anglo-Norman." *MP* 13:741–45.

Hope Emily Allen

1917

"*The Manuel des Pechiez* and the Scholastic Prologue." RR 8:434–62.

"A Note on the *Lamentation of Mary*." MP 14:255–56.

"A Note on the *Proverbs of Prophets, Poets and Saints*." MP 14:757–58.

"The *Speculum Vitae*: Addendum." PMLA 32:133–62.

1918

"The Mystical Lyrics of the *Manuel des Pechiez*." RR 9:154–93.

"The Origin of the *Ancrene Riwle*." PMLA 33:474–546.

"The *Pupilla Oculi*." MLN 33:186.

1919

"A New Latin Manuscript of the 'Ancren Riwle.'" MLR 14:209–10.

"On Richard Rolle's Lyrics." MLR 14:320–21.

1921

"The 'Ancren Riwle' and Kilburn Priory." MLR 16:316–22.

1922

"Another Latin MS of the 'Ancren Riwle.'" MLR 17:403.

1923

"Ancient Grief" [short story]. *Atlantic Monthly* 131 (February):177–87.

"A Glut of Fruit" [short story]. *Atlantic Monthly* 131 (September):343–52.

"Some Fourteenth Century Borrowings from the 'Ancren Riwle.'" MLR 18:1–8.

"A Thirteenth-Century Coronation Rubric." *Church Quarterly Review* 95: 335–41.

1924

"On 'Some Fourteenth Century Borrowings from Ancren Riwle.'" *MLR* 19:95.

"Richard Rolle" [letter]. *TLS*, May 8, p. 286.

"Richard Rolle" [letter]. *TLS*, January 8, p. 24.

1926

"A Medieval Prayer" [letter]. *Times* [London], November 16, p. 10.

1927

"The Fanciful Countryman" [short story]. *Dial* 83 (December):477–500.

Writings Ascribed to Richard Rolle, Hermit of Hampole, and Materials for His Biography. MLA Monograph Series, vol. 3. New York: D. C. Heath; London: Oxford University Press. Appeared in 1928.

1928

"Cyprus Cats" [letter]. *TLS*, August 9, p. 581.

"Richard Rolle" [letter]. *TLS*, November 22, p. 910.

1929

"Further Borrowings from 'Ancren Riwle.'" *MLR* 24:1–15.

"Lollards and English Art" [letter]. *TLS*, July 18, p. 576.

"On the Author of the *Ancren Riwle*." *PMLA* 44:635–80.

1931

"Birthplace of Richard Rolle" [letter]. *TLS*, September 10, p. 683.

The English Writings of Richard Rolle Hermit of Hampole. Oxford: Oxford University Press.

1932

"The Localization of Bodl. MS. 34." *MLR* 28:485–87.

"New Manuscripts of Richard Rolle" [letter]. *TLS*, March 17, p. 202.

"Richard Rolle" [letter]. *TLS*, July 14, p. 516.

1934

"The 'Ancren Riwle' and Geoffrey of Monmouth." *MLR* 29:173.

"Eleanor Cobham" [letter]. *TLS*, March 22, p. 214.

"A Medieval Work, Margery Kempe of Lynn" [letter]. *Times* [London], December 17, p. 15.

1935

"'Dicing Fly' and 'The Alchemist'" [letter]. *TLS*, June 27, p. 416.

"'Dicing Fly'" [correction; letter]. *TLS*, August 1, p. 489.

"A Drift of Fishers" [query]. *N&Q* 168:442–43.

"Early Modern English Dictionary" [letter]. *TLS*, May 23, p. 331.

"English 'Curds' or 'Fresh Cheese' and the Wood-Louse" [query]. *N&Q* 169:9–10.

"Influence of Superstition upon Vocabulary: Two Related Examples (Prepared from the Files of the Early Modern English Dictionary)." *PMLA* 50: 1033–46.

"The Lamb and the Flag" [query]. *N&Q* 168:334.

"'Little King,' 'Sow,' 'Lady Cow.'" *JAF* 48:191–93.

"Mysticism" [letter]. *Times* [London], January 12, p. 8.

"Superstitions Attached to the 'Black-Beetle,' 'Lobster,' 'Wood-Louse'" [query]. *N&Q* 168:460.

"The Three Daughters of Deorman." *PMLA* 50:899–902.

"The Tortington Chartulary" [letter]. *Times* [London], February 14, p. 92.

1936

"The Ancren Riwle" [letter]. *TLS*, October 24, p. 863.

"The Fifteenth-Century 'Association of Beasts, of Birds, and of Man': The Earliest Text with 'Language for Carvers' (A Note of the *Early Modern English Dictionary*)." *PMLA* 51:602–06.

"The Influence of Superstition upon Vocabulary." *PMLA* 51:904–20 (continued from *PMLA* 50:1033–46).

"Local Publication of Records and the Needs of the Philologist." *Proceedings, British Records Association*, i:33–38 (paper read November 18, 1935).

"Manuscripts of the Ancren Riwle" [letter]. *TLS*, February 8, p. 116.

1940

The Book of Margery Kempe, ed. Sanford B. Meech, with notes and appendices by Hope Emily Allen. Vol. 1. EETS, o.s., vol. 212. London: Oxford University Press.

"Wynkyn de Worde and a Second French Compilation from the 'Ancren Riwle' with a Description of the First." In *Essays and Studies in Honor of Carleton Brown*, ed. Percy W. Long. New York: New York University Press, pp. 182–219.

1941

"Bogus, Etc., A Note and Related Queries." *AN&Q* 1.

"The Book of Margery Kempe" [letter]. *TLS*, March 22, p. 139.

1942

"The Text of Trollope" [letter]. *TLS*, April 4, p. 180.

"An Oneida Tale." *JAF* 57:280–81.

"Call to a New Britain" [letter]. *TLS*, April 12, p. 171.

"Connecticut Chat." *JAF* 64:223–24.

INDEX

Index